$f\mathbf{P}$

CHANGING
the RULES

Adventures of
a Wall Street
Maverick

MURIEL SIEBERT
with Aimee Lee Ball

THE FREE PRESS   New York London Toronto Sydney Singapore

fP

THE FREE PRESS
A Division of Simon & Schuster Inc.
1230 Avenue of the Americas
New York, NY 10020

For information regarding special discounts for bulk purchases,
please contact Simon & Schuster Special Sales at 1-800-456-6798 or
business@simonandschuster.com

Designed by Karolina Harris
Manufactured in the United States of America
1 2 3 4 5 6 7 8 9 10

Library of Congress Cataloging-in-Publication Data
Siebert, Muriel
Changing the rules: adventures of a Wall Street maverick/
Muriel Siebert, with Aimee Lee Ball
p. cm.
Includes index.
1. Siebert, Muriel 2. Stockbrokers—New York (State)—New York—Biography
3. Businesswomen—New York (State)—New York—Biography
4. New York Stock Exchange—History—20th century I. Ball, Aimee Lee II. Title
HG4928.5.S58 2002
332.64'273'092—dc21
[B]   2002073847
ISBN 978-1-4165-7331-9

CONTENTS

CHANGING
the RULES

1

STREET PEOPLE

Know a lot about a little.

When I left Cleveland with five hundred dollars and a used Studebaker just before Thanksgiving 1954, I had been away from home and family only once. Travel was too extravagant and expensive in my childhood, except for the occasional over-crowded, overheated motor trip to Florida. But that one trip the previous summer was a vacation in New York City with two girl-friends.

Our teenaged excursion with a busload of other gawking tourists included the New York Stock Exchange, where a guide explained how the market was made: Trading was conducted at oak-and-brass posts called horseshoes, connected by pneumatic tubes to the stock ticker. Outside the posts stood specialists, who were expected to maintain an orderly market by buying and selling particular securities for their own accounts and by acting as agents in specific stocks. Members of the Exchange negotiated with these middlemen and with one another. If, for instance, the highest price anyone was willing to bid for "ABC Widget" was $65 and the lowest price anyone was offering for selling the stock was $66, the specialist might bid $65½ to narrow the spread between supply and demand, entering his buy and sell orders in a loose-leaf notebook.

Fines were imposed on the clerks who wrote the orders and took them to the brokers if they ran rather than walked across the imposing room, two-thirds the size of a football field, with rich Georgian marble and a five-story-high ceiling decorated in genuine gold leaf. When a broker was summoned (in this ante-diluvian time before beepers and pagers), a metal card with the number assigned to him would slide out and flap on a giant black annunciator board—as if for a customer awaiting éclairs at a crowded bakery—over the Juliet balcony where opening and closing bells were rung.

What I saw as I looked down from the visitors' gallery was a sea of men in dark suits, punctuated by the occasional pastel jacket of a runner or clerk. The wooden floor itself was literally covered with paper slips, the detritus of deal making, to be swept up at the end of the day. What I heard was the clamorous human buzz of those thousands of deals, none of it muffled by the bullet-proof glass that now protects the inhabitants of this microcosm from the public. (The glass went up after a 1967 Yip-pie protest led by Abbie Hoffman, who rained dollar bills down on the traders' heads.)

Only a few flimsy stadium-style seats that flipped up when not in use lined the walls of rather ramshackle wooden cubicles around the circumference of the room. But nobody was sitting down. Quite the contrary—the very act of standing in place seemed to constitute an isometric exercise, so inclined to motion did everyone seem. I didn't understand any of the arcane two- or three-letter symbols for the companies scrolling by on the "black box" ticker, but I realized that every one of them represented a transaction taking place—perhaps a hundred shares, perhaps a million.

I never had a strategy, no long-term game plan. But after absorbing all that fierce energy, I turned to my friends and said, "Now, *this* is exciting. Maybe I'll come back here and look for a job." At that time, tourists were given a piece of ticker tape printed with their name as a souvenir. I still have the few inches of worn and faded tape that said, "Welcome to the NYSE, Muriel Siebert."

Turns out I wasn't so welcome after all.

. . .

There really was a wall at Wall Street, although it was actually more of a wooden stockade—built by the Dutch when New York was Nieuw Amsterdam—to keep the villagers' goats and hogs from straying into the surrounding countryside, and to protect their trading post from the pushy British, who managed to take over anyway. The Street became synonymous with finance in 1792, when the New York Stock Exchange was established according to a set of rules known as the Buttonwood Agreement, named for a tree on lower Wall Street where business was often conducted. Twenty-four prominent brokers and merchants, in powdered wigs and waistcoats, agreed to trade public stock—bidding on only one at a time—and to bet on foreign battles, elections and cockfights, thus creating the world's most exclusive boys' club.

There was no actual wall to scale 175 years later, when I made the Stock Exchange coed. Although I purchased a "seat" on December 28, 1967, there was no place to sit down, either. The symbolic description is a throwback to the days when brokers sat at tables on the trading floor. I'd been told that there might be media coverage to witness the swearing in of the first woman on the New York Stock Exchange, and I considered having my hair done and makeup professionally applied, but the NYSE elected not to allow TV cameras or reporters into the boardroom where it took place. Friends and family are not invited—the occasion is more pro forma than inaugural or even ceremonial—and the Board of Governors had decided to treat me like anyone else being sworn in, which was fine by me.

The moment my hands really shook was when I signed the register. There's a lot of history in that book. It's huge—about nine inches thick, with the entire constitution of the Stock Exchange written in longhand and the signatures of everyone who's ever been a member. I saw names from the Civil War, when the country was saddled with several billion dollars of

debt and Wall Street was the place to trade it. The volume literally overflowed to the street—the origin of the Curb Exchange,
which later evolved into the American Stock Exchange. I saw
names from the outbreak of World War I and the ensuing economic panic, when the NYSE actually had to close in August
1914. It reopened six months later, only after Europeans started
sending gold to this country for safekeeping. Our country's nascent promises of free enterprise and prosperity to more than a
century and a half of immigrants were written in the white
spaces between the names.

The only tangible memento of that memorable day was an
oval white metallic badge, approximately the size of a political
button, with my name printed in black and the number 2646 in
red. I received it about six months later. There was a clip on the
back meant to fit the breast pocket of a man's suit. I spoke to a
jeweler about converting it, but I was furious at the price named
for such an adjustment and ended up fastening it with a safety
pin. I guess he felt entitled to charge me $11.50 when told that
the badge had cost me $445,000. It was by far the most expensive
piece of jewelry I owned or would ever own, and I wondered
what it would look like on a formal gown.

Not long after my bid card was accepted, a note arrived from an
elderly gentleman who remembered a Broadway musical more
than fifty years earlier called *The Wall Street Girl*. A popular ac-
tress of the day named Blanche Ring starred as a "brokeress"
whose investment in a Nevada mining company saves her father
from financial embarrassment. Will Rogers played the rope-
twirling Lariat Bill, and Ms. Ring sang a song called "I Should
Have Been a Boy." A review of the play noted: "She puts through
some vastly successful financial deals, the like of which, if they
were actual, would make real Wall Street quiver with excitement."

The Wall Street Girl opened at Geo. M. Cohan's Theatre on
April 15, 1912—the same day that a new steel ship weighing
nearly fifty thousand tons called the *Titanic* sank in the icy
waters of the northern Atlantic. I hoped it was not a bad omen.

• • •

My older sister was already living in New York, divorced and working in public relations, when I arrived in 1954, several credits shy of a degree from Flora Stone Mather College, the women's division of Case Western Reserve, where my father had gone to dental school. Women were expected to study teaching or nursing, but I decided to take a course in money and banking at the men's college—I was the only woman, and the teacher would call on me as "the delegate from Mather." But in the early 1950s, my father became ill with what was generally referred to, obliquely and in hushed voices, as "the big C." His brother, a doctor who held the lease on my father's office, had him evicted, installing as tenant his own son, a dentist who assumed my father's practice (my first experience with a hostile takeover). This was the same "Uncle Doc" who billed his mother for medical counsel when he visited her in the nursing home and was off getting an honor from his Masonic lodge when my dying father was calling for him.

The dying was happening during my junior year at college, and my only respite was playing bridge, a pastime that became so all-consuming that I didn't bother to graduate (although I got master points in bridge). At the funeral, Uncle Doc's sisters (Aunt Rena, Aunt Flo and Aunt Shirley) refused to speak with their brother. My father's $5,000 insurance policy paid for the burial expense, but several years of medical bills had eaten up his savings. There was no other estate.

And there were few job prospects for me when I arrived in New York. I applied at the United Nations, where my cousin Alvin Roseman was one of the U.S. representatives, and at Merrill Lynch, which I remembered from my visit as the biggest brokerage on the Exchange. Both prospective employers turned me down—the United Nations because I didn't speak two languages and Merrill Lynch because I didn't have a college degree. On my next interview, at Bache & Co., I lied about my degree

and was offered two positions: The accounting department paid
$75 a week; the research department paid only $65, but it
sounded more interesting.

As a trainee first assigned to the wire desk, my responsibility
was taking telexes to the senior analysts from Bache brokers in
out-of-town branches who had questions on behalf of individual clients or institutions—pension funds, mutual funds, bank
trust funds, college endowments and foundations—wanting to
know: What do you think of General Electric? Should we buy or
sell General Motors?

The institutional investor was a relatively new breed on Wall
Street. Some were limited to a legal list of government securities
and corporate bonds; others had more leeway to buy common
stocks but were restricted to quality lists. (The blue chips then
were companies such as U.S. Steel and Standard Oil.) Certainly
no institutions were investing in the small technology stocks of
the day. Until the 1950s, many financial bodies, traditionally
guided by prudence, considered the stock market too wily and
mercurial. Recognition of the usefulness of potentially higher-
return assets happily coincided with my own arrival on the Street.

I was really a glorified gofer, but you create opportunities by
performing, not complaining. I paid attention and picked up on
why the experts liked a particular company or industry. Analyzing the market is both an art and a science. The financial data
that indicate how a company fits into the economy make up the
science part; seeing a pattern in those numbers and then looking

---

You create opportunities by performing, not complaining.

---

ahead is an art. From the beginning, the recondite world of figures seemed like second nature to me. At college, I didn't have to
do any homework in my accounting courses and still could ace
the exams because I could look at a page of numbers, and they
would light up like a Broadway marquee.

After six weeks at Bache, I was given a raise of five dollars a week, which meant an extra twenty cents a day for lunch and a new apartment in the former maids' quarters of a Park Avenue building, reached by the freight elevator. (My sister got the one small bedroom; I slept on a couch in the living room from a furniture store called Foamland.) Trainees were required to use opinions generated by the company elders, who all had special bailiwicks of responsibility. Any time the market got tough, research looked like an expendable commodity, and when an analyst left a brokerage, he was not replaced—his industries were reassigned to someone else in the office. When business improved, the senior people were allowed to lighten their load by dumping what was considered a "doggy industry" on one of the trainees.

Sometimes the one who gets dumped on gets the goods. Werner Baer, the man in charge of chemicals and drugs, had been given radio, TV and motion pictures, but he wasn't interested in those businesses, so I inherited them. A distinguished veteran analyst named Henry Van Ells had responsibility for transportation—everything that moved on land or sea or air— but his heart was really with the railroads. He knew every line, every mile of track, where every boxcar could be found, and his

---

Sometimes the one who gets dumped on gets the goods.

---

language was peppered with railroad slang and the colorful nicknames assigned to rail stocks based on the company's name or ticker symbol. (Delaware, Lackawanna & Western Railroad was known as "Delay, Linger and Wait.") Jet aircraft had been invented during the Second World War (the Boeing 707 was adapted from the air force jet), but Van Ells didn't believe there was much future in airlines—didn't think the companies could even finance the next round of equipment—so, despite my total lack of background or interest in aviation, he gave me that industry to learn and cover. The following year, turboprop aircraft were introduced. It wasn't long before jets revitalized the industry, and eventually commercial jets came along. I was at the threshold of a major chapter in economic history.

Van Ells knew the people, the history and the statistics of the industry he covered, and he could make a shrewd guess as to the future performance of every rail line in the nation. He taught me that it was necessary to learn everything possible about a company, to let the numbers tell the story. The depreciation and cash flow I had learned in accounting classes became much more valuable than any interpretation of *Beowulf* or conjugation of Latin verbs. And having my "own" industry entitled me to attend noon meetings of the New York Society of Security Analysts. The Coachman Restaurant would send up food, and the waiters would hang around hoping for tips (the information kind).

My motto was: Know a lot about a little. I zeroed in on fifteen to twenty companies and really delved into my subject, spending time with executives and keeping up to date on all contracts, cancellations, slowdowns and bids. I tried to study everything there was to know about management, production, suppliers, competition, research and labor conditions. If a company had a disappointing quarter, I could figure out whether it was a systemic problem in the organization or something beyond its control. Companies were willing to provide information to in-

Know a lot about a little.

vestors, large or small, but they weren't going to blurt out everything. You've got to know the right questions to produce the right answers. As Hamlet put it: By indirections find directions out. A senior officer of a company I was analyzing once said to me, "There's something in the back of your head that you want answered. Gradually it will dawn on me what you're really after, and you might not even know it yourself." It wasn't hard to put two and two together and come up with four. When I analyzed United Airlines, I was just one penny off the company's own internal estimates.

There were one or two other female analysts in my firm and several on the Street, but they were generally given "ladylike" industries such as food or cosmetics or retail, since of course women were supposed to be good at cooking and shopping. One

---

You've got to know the right questions to produce the right answers.

---

woman who covered drugs was a winner with the company that developed the birth control pill. I was certainly the only woman reading *Civil Aeronautics Board Reports* and *Missile and Space Daily* in the beauty parlor.

The leaders of the aviation industry then were mythical figures known far beyond the business world, comparable to Bill Gates today. Juan Trippe, the founder and then president of Pan American World Airways, had begun his career on Wall Street as a bond salesman. But he'd been in love with flying ever since boyhood, when his father took him to an air race between the Wright Brothers and their lifelong competitor Glenn Curtiss. Trippe started his first endeavor, Long Island Airways, by purchasing five navy-surplus single-engine floatplanes for five hundred dollars each in 1923. He financed the new airline by selling stock to his Yale classmates. The company flew to Atlantic City and other vacation spots, and Trippe handled every aspect of the business, from keeping the books to carrying the bags.

Cyrus Rowlett Smith, the president of American Airlines, came to the aviation business in the days of open-cockpit biplanes. Working from the age of nine as office boy to a Texas cattleman, he was also a cotton picker and bank teller until being hired at an accounting firm whose client was launching and absorbing small airlines. Named president of the newly formed American in 1934 (and known to everyone in the organization as "Mr. C.R."), he helped design the DC-3, the work-horse of passenger planes in the 1930s and 1940s, and led American into the jet age with the introduction of the first nonstop transcontinental jet service in 1959.

One of the legends of the industry was Captain Eddie Rickenbacker, the celebrated air ace of World War I, who was running Eastern Airlines. He was scheduled to come in for one of the research meetings that Bache held every Wednesday with the salespeople and senior partners. I had been at the firm about six months, and the airline industry was now mine, under the guidance of Van Ells, so I was entitled to pose some questions. In those days, analysts were more polite and less probing, but I broached some touchy subjects. Several heads turned disapprovingly to see who was giving this demigod of aviation such a hard time. I had read in a footnote of Eastern's annual report that the company depreciated its aircraft three different ways: five years for taxes, four years for stockholders, seven years internally. (This accounting strategy is all legal, but no company wants to deal with taxes in any but the most aggressive fashion.) It didn't occur to me to be timid, not even when facing the tall, commanding figure of Rickenbacker.

"Captain," I said, "I've figured out the company's earnings three ways, based on the three different depreciation schedules."

"Young lady," he replied, "are you permanently employed? If not, there's a job for you at Eastern Airlines."

I declined. The Street still had allure, even though it wasn't paved with gold. After getting another raise I became the first of the trainees to earn one hundred dollars a week. Bache had a policy that any employee who hit that mark was taken off the time clock, but the bosses knew that the other trainees would realize what I was making, so they took *everybody* off the clock. I doubled my salary in two years, was earning $130 a week and living much better, but I was still way behind the men at the firm and knew I'd have to change jobs to make any significant headway. At my request, the "Captain" introduced me to two of his bankers: Hugh Knowlton at Kuhn, Loeb & Co. and William Barclay Harding at Smith Barney. Appointments were arranged at both firms, but neither had ever employed a woman as anything but a secretary, and they weren't about to hire a female analyst. One interviewer said I'd be prohibited from going out of town to represent the company; the other said I'd have to wear a hat and white gloves in the elevator like the rest of the "girls."

My analysis was showing a potential profit in the fact that different air carriers had opposite and thus complementary seasonal traffic patterns. Those flying to Florida needed all kinds of capacity from November to April, while those flying transatlantic were busiest from May through October. With all the airlines reequipping, I had the idea of a leasing company that would buy the planes and enter into long-term contracts with the carriers that needed them for their seasonal use. Bache didn't have a new business department to develop such an ambitious project, so I asked for and received permission to take the idea to the investment house of Loeb Rhodes & Co. For a while, it looked as if my idea was a "go" project that we'd work on together, and one of the partners suggested that there was a job for me there. Thinking I had a firm offer, I foolishly told my bosses at Bache that I wasn't happy and was asked to leave the same day. But the job at Loeb Rhodes didn't come through, and I found myself unemployed. What's more, the long-term leasing plan fell through because the airlines couldn't agree on the configuration of the cockpit.

Sending my résumé around the Street didn't produce a single response. When the placement bureau of the New York Society of Security Analysts sent out the same résumé using my initials rather than my first name, M. F. Siebert got an interview—and a job—in the research department of Shields & Co., for $9,500 a year. It was 1958, and this somewhat enlightened brokerage permitted a female analyst to travel, but even more important, I could follow any company in any industry. One of my reports was about a conglomerate called Ogden that was planning to spin off a lucrative subsidiary called Syntex, a drug division that had produced some of the original allergy medicines. For every two shares of Ogden a stockholder owned, he'd be allowed to buy one share of Syntex at two dollars. That made it a tax-free transaction for both company and stockholder.

One day on the subway, I bumped into another woman who had worked in sales at Bache. "What do you like?" she asked. I told her that I was recommending Ogden. She took that idea up to Ed Merkle, president of the Madison Fund, and when I got to Shields, he called me to say that Madison had made money on my report and therefore owed me an order. Problem was, I wasn't licensed to sell, wasn't *supposed* to sell, had never *tried* to sell. I went into the office of the partner in charge of research and asked, "Shall I wait until I get registered?" He practically shoved me out the door. "Go get the order," he said, "and we'll make it up to you at Christmas."

The Stock Exchange takes a very dim view of selling stocks or soliciting orders without being authorized. In order to get a license, you must be sponsored by a member firm and take the General Securities Registered Representative License, also known as Series 7. The extent of my ignorance was vast. For the first time I had to learn exactly what a broker can and cannot say about a stock. I learned about "call options" and "put options" (the right to buy or sell a specific amount of a stock or commodity); about "margin requirements" (the amount that must be deposited in an account before buying securities with borrowed money, using the shares as collateral); about "selling short" (borrowing a security from a broker and selling it with the understanding that it will be bought back later, hopefully at a lower price, and returned to the broker). Fortunately my college course on money and banking had been a primer on the Federal Reserve Board. The nation's central bank controls the money supply by setting margin requirements for credit extended by brokers and dealers to investors, setting interest rates that banks pay for borrowed funds, and buying and selling government securities on the open market. Simply stated, when the Fed tightens money, interest rates tend to go up because the demand for money exceeds the supply; when the Fed eases up, interest rates tend to go down.

Sometimes a partner in the firm would call me trying to unload a block of stock on one of the clients who relied on my research. I'd say, "Look, Madison Fund expects me to know what I'm recommending. Why don't I get the annual report and

Realizing that I was underpaid gave me the gumption to move on.

visit the company tomorrow?" I knew perfectly well that there wasn't time for all that—the block would be gone by then or given to another firm to sell. But I wasn't going to jeopardize my relationship with clients simply because it was expedient and profitable for the firm, and for me. Analysis took time.

That was just one of my continuing frustrations. After a year at Shields, I had brought in National Aviation and several other funds, but I was still making just $9,500 a year, plus 20 percent of the commissions I generated. Two guys hired straight out of B-school were put on salary at $8,800. One of my fellow analysts knew of my mounting irritation and informed the partners, who called me in and asked, "If we raise you to $12,500, would that make you happy?" But a male colleague doing the same work was making more than $20,000, which the partners justified because he was a man with a family. That's take-a-vacation money or buy-a-new-car money or start-investing-your-own-money money. Realizing that I was underpaid gave me the gumption to move on.

My reports regularly appeared in a weekly investment advisory newsletter put out by a Shields analyst named Walter K. Gutman, who was known as the Proust of Wall Street. He had the ability to describe something technological, such as lasers, in accessible, vivid lay language, and his newsletter, a blend of fact, opinion and philosophy, was widely followed, hot as a pistol but a little half cracked. In mid-1960 Gutman told me that he was planning to start his own firm with Teddy Rosen, who headed sales at Burnham (later to become the beleaguered Drexel Burnham Lambert), and Roland B. Stearns, who was running Stearns & Co., a small firm that already had a Stock Exchange seat. (His father was one of the founding partners of Bear Stearns, but that firm had a policy of not hiring relatives.) I was asked to come in as a partner. When the rumor got out, I was fired at Shields.

The minute I lost my job, a colleague named Green called Madison Fund to get the account. Ed Merkle, president of the fund, phoned me to say, "I didn't know you were fired. There's an office here you can use until the new firm gets started, and I think you should be sitting in the room when Mr. Green comes in next Tuesday." It was actually a rather clever little plan for showing me support while keeping the door open for any business Shields might still bring his way. And Green looked satisfyingly miserable when he saw me. Merkle became a lifelong friend, and I repaid his many kindnesses any way I could. He had asked for contributions to help rebuild his church, and years later, at his funeral, the pastor came up to introduce himself. "I wanted to meet you," he said and pointed at a beautiful stained-glass window. "You paid for that."

When plans for the new firm were announced in the Stock Exchange *Weekly Bulletin,* I got a call from a friend at Goodbody Stockbrokers, where Gutman had worked, warning that he would be blackballed as an allied member because he was too controversial. One rumor was that he had gone to the brokerage with his girlfriend, who was black; interracial dating, in those times, was not thought of benevolently. The warning turned out to be dead on: Gutman's NYSE application was turned down. Instead of becoming a senior partner in a new firm, he was hired to head the research department at Stearns & Co., where *I* became a partner. The coup de grâce came when Gutman published a nasty diatribe against a policeman who'd ticketed him for driving—with Jack Kerouac as a passenger, no less—with an open bottle of wine in the convertible. Gutman unwisely printed the cop's badge number and advised him to be more respectful in the future. I was the partner who got called down to the Exchange and was told in no uncertain terms to supervise and edit what he wrote.

One of Gutman's December 1960 newsletters recommended U.S. Photo Supply Corp., a company that claimed exclusive American distribution rights to a French device for making prints from negatives in ten seconds in normal daylight—a breakthrough in amateur photography. The stock became a "hot issue" in the bear market of 1961, taking off in an almost perpendicular rise in price from $2.50 to $105. But in 1962, as part of a broader investigation into the financial markets, the Securities and Exchange Commission (SEC) claimed that Stearns had "pushed" the stock and that relatives of several men in the firm (including Gutman's son and former wife) had purchased stock, through discretionary accounts, before the investment letter got out. Then they had sold their shares at a large profit in the swift market that followed. In a heated exchange with the SEC lawyer, Roland Stearns testified that he had been "away for Christmas" during the time in question but that my analysis was chiefly responsible for recommending the stock to customers. No longer restricted to following aviation, I had become enthused about electronics, and I thought that if the ten-second wonder worked in real life as it did in a controlled environment, the company would have been a major player. But when the device was demonstrated at a press conference, it basically curled up and died. By the time of the SEC probe, the stock price had dropped below one dollar.

Company policy, Stearns said, permitted insiders to buy Gutman-recommended stocks but required that any such purchase be held for at least a week after the market letter came out. But he admitted that it was the U.S. Photo transactions that had demonstrated the need for such a policy. Until then, there had

been a "hedge clause" in fine print at the end of the market letter
that seemed to be license for Stearns officials to make use of the
information any way they chose. It read: "In the general course
of business, partners and/or employees may or may not have a
position, long or short, in the securities mentioned and from
time to time may be executing buy and/or sell orders for themselves and/or their customers." The Gutman newsletter was dis-
continued that spring, citing "belt-pinching," and at the end of
the year Stearns was censured by the SEC for "conduct inconsis-
tent with just and equitable principles of trade."

The decline and fall of U.S. Photo and the subsequent SEC
investigation got a lot of coverage in the many New York newspapers published at the time. I was not subpoenaed and had no
real fear of personal recrimination: even though I had bought
some of the stock myself, I hadn't traded it. (The worthless
stock certificates are still stuck in a desk drawer somewhere.)
And I had left Stearns. The firm's potential for growth was
impeded when Gutman was blackballed and Teddy Rosen
decided to stay where he was. I was one of only a few female
partners on the Street, but my philosophy differed from that of
my partners. They were interested in speculative hot stocks; I
wanted to concentrate on larger, more substantial companies,
like airlines and the aerospace industry. But I was finding no welcome mat rolled out for me when I looked for another job.

I had been doing some volunteer work with the Henry Street
Settlement on Manhattan's Lower East Side, working with the
children of recent immigrants. We read to them, taught them
how to play baseball and Ping-Pong, tried to help them accli-
mate to American customs. Henry Street was a favorite charity
of several young Wall Streeters—perhaps because so many of
our parents and grandparents had come to this country similarly
overwhelmed by the strangeness of a new land. One of the people my own age whom I met there was Mark Finkle, son of
David Finkle, who had been a senior partner at Bear Stearns and
left to start an eponymous brokerage. Mark had no interest in

dealing with clients himself, the glad-handing, entertaining, schmoozing part of the work—he wanted to be on the floor trading. He went to his father with the suggestion that I join Finkle & Co., which had no analyst. "She's clean as a whistle," he said, "and these firms are being unfair to her." I was offered 40 percent commissions plus 5 percent of the partnership's pre-tax profit.

It was tradition that when a broker changed firms, former clients would put in a "good will order." On my first day at my new job, I got an order that netted a commission of $2,000.

"Isn't this great?" I said to David Finkle.

"That's shit," he said evenly.

It was at Finkle that I learned that "crossing the block" did not mean darting across Fifth Avenue to get a closer look at Bergdorf Goodman's windows: Davey Finkle was on the executive committee of the old Chicago & Northwestern Railroad Company, where he'd helped a man named Ben Heinemann get control of the company. Chicago & Northwestern wanted to buy a railroad called Gulf, Mobil & Ohio. Finkle was trying to persuade institutions to buy GM&O and to vote in favor of the sellout to Chicago & Northwestern. When I looked in a publication called *Vickers* that listed the holdings of all mutual funds and other institutions, I saw that the Channing Fund owned a block of GM&O. One of Channing's directors was Tom Lenaugh, then the treasurer of the Ford Foundation. He was the head of research at Goodbody who'd warned me that Gutman would be blackballed. I called Lenaugh, said I'd like to talk to the fund's portfolio manager and was told to call Norman Walker. GM&O stock was selling at $22 a share, but Channing's investment committee had voted its stock for sale at a higher price of $24. Walker said that if I found a buyer at that price, I could have the order and the block of stock. That meant finding a buyer willing to pay "over the market," or more than it was selling for at the time, in order to get a good-sized block.

Wally Bowman, who was running Delaware Income Fund,

was interested but never bought anything unless he met with the management. So I flew out to Chicago and together we went to see Ben Heinemann. I'd done my homework to figure out how efficient the operation was, how the new acquisition would fit in, whether Chicago & Northwestern would be adding new tracks, what kind of service it would offer, whether anybody else was offering that service already and whether the acquisition would produce savings. When we left Heinemann's office, Bowman said, "I'll take the block at $24." Delaware Fund gave us a big enough order to bid GM&O up to the price where Channing had authorized the sale. Finkle "crossed the block," meaning that we handled both the buy and the sell, earning commissions on both parts of the deal. I made about $8,000 that day, which was a lot of money. At the time, I was paying $185 for a studio apartment with a raised dinette and good closet space overlooking the courts at the Town Tennis Club.

The next day, Davey Finkle was clearly interested in my Rolodex. "How do you know these people?" he asked.

"From the New York Society of Security Analysts," I said. "I'm head of the airlines committee."

"You come sit here next to me," he said, pointing to the trading table. That's where I learned a new language consisting mainly of four-letter words. Traders were from different backgrounds, with different pressures than the analysts, who tended to be more refined. These were Damon Runyanesque characters, known to throw telephones or yank cords out of the wall if things didn't go their way. Under their tutelage, I soon became an expert in vulgarity. But I also learned how to trade stocks and saw that I could make serious money by getting the whole order instead of a small payment for research. Finkle would call people he knew and say, "Listen, I'm sending you my partner. She's a girl, but she can still pick up the lunch check." To me, he'd say, "Don't speak to the analysts. Speak to the portfolio managers because they'll think of you down the line, and you'll get the orders. Speak to the traders because they give out the orders, and if they don't think you're capable, you won't get the business even if the portfolio manager recommends it." He would tell me to call so-and-so, and I'd ask what I was going to call so-and-so about. His typical response: "Aw, I don't give a fuck, just call him."

Sometimes he'd grab the phone out of my hand and tell me I didn't know how to close a sale. He had grown up at Bear Stearns as a bond trader and ending up owning a big chunk of the firm because of his production, making bids on blocks of bonds and moving them from customer to customer. If, say, Metropolitan Life Insurance Company had $20 million of bonds to sell—maybe for reasons that had nothing to do with the value of the bond; maybe to buy a piece of real estate—the firms on the Street would make bids for the block. When the pension plans were growing and starting to buy common stock, Finkle was instrumental in getting Bear Stearns to make bids on blocks of stock, just as the firm did on bonds, sometimes buying a piece and putting it in the firm's trading account in order to facilitate the deal.

With bonds, brokers didn't need numbers about a company's earnings or revenues because bond-rating agencies did all that work, based on debt coverage and other kinds of information. I once heard Finkle call up Brother Parker, who founded the Put-nam Fund. This was the entire conversation from beginning to end: "I got this block of XYZ stock. I don't know shit from pound cake about the earnings. All I know is it sells for twenty dollars, and it pays a dollar and a half dividend. You'll take the block, Brother? Fine." He expected me to cross a block like that too. But I had come up as an analyst, and clients counted on me to know the companies. Finkle had little use for analysts. "Who needs 'em?" he'd snarl. "In a bull market, everything goes up, and in a bear market, they break you."

My heart pounded when I had to call on the men who were responsible for investing such enormous sums of money. I was not a natural salesperson, and I'm a disaster on names. I remem-ber numbers. Often the men were embarrassed when I picked up a check—they'd suddenly become acutely interested in the bottoms of their briefcases or else go to the bathroom. But I knew the product I was selling, and I learned how to convey information with clarity, authority and brevity. Gerry Tsai, a former analyst at Bache who was managing Fidelity Capital Fund, once said, "If you can't tell me why I should buy or sell a stock in a page and a half, you don't know the company." And I had a knack for cutting through trivia. A potential client can be overwhelmed by too much detail and consequently be indecisive in making a commitment.

The first stock I really pushed was Boeing. When everyone else was saying "Sell," I was telling clients to buy, and the institutions that bought it tripled their money. Boeing already had the 707 jet (a commercial edition of the military jet tanker) and the three-engine 727. The new 737 was a two-engine jet that

---

"If you can't tell me why I should buy or sell a stock in a page and a half, you don't know the company."

---

could get into smaller airports and could make money with fewer passengers. What made me take a stand on the company was a senior official from United Airlines telling me that the Boeing plane had passed every performance test it had been given on the day it was delivered. Terry Drinkwater, who was running Western Airlines, actually gave me the brochure showing the interchangeable spare parts that could be used for different planes in the fleet, thus lowering the operating costs. ("I know you're going to ask me for this," he said, "so I might as well give it to you.") Today that might be called insider information, but I considered it doing my homework. I studied companies from every possible angle, and I talked to customers, suppliers and engineers, but some of my best recommendations were based on what the SEC now calls the "knowing possession" of material nonpublic information.

Rudd-Melikian Corporation in Philadelphia had invented the coffee vending machine under the name Kwik Kafe. Stearns had brought the company public, and I placed a lot of the stock with institutional clients, including the Madison Fund, which had given me my first order. The underwriter of an initial public offering, or IPO, having raised the cash, usually gets the privilege of putting somebody on the board of directors to watch its investment, and I was elected. Some months later, there was a

---

A potential client can be overwhelmed by too much detail and consequently be indecisive in making a commitment.

---

new board member named C. Stanley Allen, who had been chairman of National Cash Register. He introduced himself by saying, "Call me Chick." One day I got a call from an analyst at T. Rowe Price, the money manager that runs mutual funds, which had bought Rudd-Melikian on my advice and was concerned that the company's payables were late. If the bills weren't being paid on time, it meant trouble. At the next meeting of the board, I asked a lot of questions but could not figure out what was wrong: The company's assets and liabilities showed plenty of cash to meet obligations. But if something smells, there might be a dead fish somewhere.

The next day I sent a registered letter to Mr. Rudd and Mr. Melikian asking for a breakdown of assets on the balance sheet. They finally admitted that there was nothing collateralizing their IOUs to the company, which were on their balance sheets as current receivables. In other words, they had lied, and the balance sheet was not as strong. When the auditing firm of Coopers & Lybrand certified the financial statements, it should have checked if the company's IOUs were backed by the collateral described, but it hadn't. (It turned out that Madison Fund and Rudd-Melikian both used Coopers & Lybrand—the former in New York, the latter in Philadelphia. Ironically, the investment company had a loss because of the sloppy accounting of the auditor's other branch.)

Mr. Call-me-Chick Allen resigned from the board immediately and said to me, "Young lady, if you're smart, you will get out of here with me." I was not sophisticated enough to know what my fiscal responsibility was; depending on the state where a broker is chartered, this sort of situation could land a person in the middle of a lawsuit. But I had clients who owned a lot of stock and sold it at tremendous losses. I had an obligation. Madison had the biggest outside holding in Rudd-Melikian, but the fund never would have bought the stock if the balance sheet hadn't been good. And if I didn't have a gut feeling about analyzing the balance sheet, I never would have found out about the crooks. Madison ultimately held the stock for years, never suing because of the shared accounting firm, and Rudd-Melikian was later merged out for very little money.

When Call-me-Chick Allen came onto the board of Rudd-Melikian, I had looked at National Cash Register's annual report and saw that it depreciated its computers fast: the first year, 40 percent; the second year, 30 percent; the third year, 20 percent; and the fourth year, 10 percent. That method is called a four-year "sum-of-the-digits," and any revenue after the four years was all profit, with no depreciation expenses. I played around with the numbers and said to Allen, "You know, NCR looks cheap." He had never encouraged my interest in the company, but one day he said, "You might be right. Maybe you should go out to Ohio and visit NCR." It was rather pleasant going to my home state to meet the chairman of a national corporation. I had looked at every available piece of public information about the company and had a list of questions that I still wanted answered. The answers confirmed my numbers. NCR was not in the forefront of new technology, but it did have a lot of computers in the field. I started to recommend the stock because the earnings were going to pop as the computers that were installed became fully depreciated. But I wouldn't have earned much if I had just gotten a lousy research chit.

If I started recommending a stock, I called the institutions that already had holdings in that company to see if they wanted to buy more before I called accounts that didn't own it. When I had an order to buy, I would call the institutions that didn't want to buy more, in the event that they wanted to sell. Then I could get the order and cross the block. Chase Manhattan Bank had a large piece of NCR but didn't want any more. One day I was told, "We've just voted the sale of the stock. Come in with a bid, and it's yours." I'd never met Jack Bridgewood, the man who ran the entire investment department at Chase, but I called him, explained how NCR's earnings were going to increase sharply because of the depreciation schedule and advised him not to sell the stock but to buy more. An hour later I got a call from Joe Debe, the head transportation analyst at Chase, who was on the investment committee.

"What did you do?" he asked. "Bridgewood just came into the meeting and unvoted the sale."

Jim Lane, who ran many of the largest corporate pension plans, was in on the meeting and asked, "Who is this Siebert, God?"

"No," said Bridgewood, "she just knows more about the company than we do."

I probably lost $200,000 in commission on that NCR sale, but the next time I called Chase, I had a customer—and a friend. The friendship would prove invaluable when I wanted to join the Big Board.

Pretty early on in my career, I realized that some of what was good for the goose would be good for the gander—that several of the stocks I researched for institutions would be good investments for me, if I only had the money. A client once asked if I owned any of the stocks I was recommending. When I said I didn't have that kind of capital, he introduced me to a loan officer at Irving Trust Company who arranged for me to borrow against what I was buying, always asking about my purchases and making similar ones himself. I imagine I helped him accumulate a tidy sum because in three or four years, I ran a $500 investment into $500,000 equity. If you're buying with borrowed money, it doesn't mean it's your money. In the sudden bear market of 1962, when President John F. Kennedy told the steel companies to roll back their prices, the market broke and my profit disappeared—all but $20,000. If you owe money in securities you've purchased, the bank isn't the loser, you are. I vowed I would never be fully hocked again.

I had some money of my own to invest when I became a partner at the brokerage firm Brimberg & Co. There I was paid 45 percent of the commissions I generated, which were about $600,000 a year. The iconoclastic and gargantuan Robert Brimberg was the real "Scarsdale Fats" of the pseudonymous Adam Smith's best-selling 1976 book *The Money Game*. Partners at the firm had placed a scale by his desk as a silent reproach, but it did no good. I'd go to a breakfast meeting with him and have my half grapefruit, my stinky poached egg and dry rye toast, while

---

If you're buying with borrowed money, it doesn't mean it's your money.

---

he'd have pancakes with a quarter pound of butter, syrup in between and scrambled eggs on top. Brimberg was known for inviting big portfolio managers to informal lunches at the office, seating them on metal folding chairs at plastic tables, plying them with corned beef and meatballs—and a little booze—while gleaning information about what they were buying and selling. ("Adam Smith" estimated that if all the funds in a group and all the trusts in a department were counted, the eight or ten guys in the room reaching for deviled eggs and pickles represented a shade under $9 billion, which, in those days, was real money.) In three years at Brimberg & Co., I gained ten pounds and a ton of knowledge, like the legitimate investment reasons why one institution might buy a stock while another would sell at the same time: A fund could be changing holdings in an industry, could have different investment objectives, could have holdings that no longer qualified as income stock or could need to take a profit to pay capital gains to holders.

Brimberg was an artist at picking up nuggets that could be used to his advantage, and everyone on the Street envied his skill. If you could find out what the big boys were up to, and he could, all you had to do was play follow-the-leader and call other money managers, who would often buy or sell the same stock. Money handlers of this ilk dealt in such gigantic blocks that any move they made could affect prices, up or down. The portfolio managers

---

If you owe money in securities you've purchased, the bank isn't the loser, *you* are.

---

loved this informal way of talking with peers. The rule was: everything off the record, no names. Just "Hey, Joe, I see you bought some utilities last week at the bottom" or "Where's the market going?" or "What three stocks do you like?" And there were fascinating guests, politicians such as Senators Birch Bayh and Eugene McCarthy, who liked the honorariums and the chance to meet the people who were running the country's big money pools.

Brimberg's wealthy father was a furrier then working at the brokerage. He had special permission from the NYSE to keep a bottle of Scotch in his desk—for his heart condition. Maybe it was the fur dynasty, but Brimberg thought that I lived too frugally and didn't dress well. He offered to take me shopping and wanted to put up half the cost of a diamond bracelet that cost $35,000 if I paid the other half. "Let me manage your money," he insisted. "At every top I'm worth more than you are."

"But at every bottom I'm worth more than you are," I

answered. "And I don't have parents like Louis and Bessie to bail
me out."

During the three years we were partners, Brimberg and I never
had a serious disagreement, and when I told him I was leaving, he
offered me the supreme compliment of saying he would put my
name on the firm: Brimberg, Siebert & Co. Even though my income and commissions were growing nicely, I wanted to be at a
larger firm. The big man worked round the clock and always wondered why I didn't want to socialize with clients on weekends.
But he worked—and literally ate—himself to death: he died in a
restaurant.

By the mid-1960s, security analysts had become Wall Street's
darlings. The booming bull market, an increased institutional
interest in common stocks, the appetite for information and the
ability to generate complex computerized evaluations trans-
formed the stature of the analyst. Since 1963, anyone who
passed an exam acquired an impressive-sounding set of initials:
CFA, for Chartered Financial Analyst. It was the era of the "selling analyst," some of whom were breaking off and starting their
own firms. Even old-line members of the Stock Exchange turned
their efforts to research for the fastest-growing segment of customers: the institutional investors. Between 1964 and 1969, the
number of active funds doubled, and knowledgeable observers
claimed that somewhere in America there was a fund with an
investment strategy to fit any customer's appetite for risk. Some
highly regarded firms even started recruiting analysts from the
ranks of the industries being researched, taking the approach
that insider understanding was incomparably valuable. Geolo-
gists were becoming oil analysts; drug marketers were becoming
health care analysts. But that word *insider* was also becoming a
pejorative. If an analyst was brought in from the underwriting
department of a corporate client, it was referred to as coming in
"over the wall," since legally these two departments were sup-

posed to be kept separate (as if by a Chinese wall) because of the potential conflict of interest, and the analyst was not to provide opinions on the corporation involved.

Long before the insider trading scandals of the 1980s, new rules to promote the full and fair disclosure of information evolved from a case the SEC brought against the Texas Gulf Sulphur Company. A court ruled that top officers and directors of the firm had violated securities laws by conducting transactions in their stock without telling the public what they knew about a rich Canadian minerals strike the company had made. The SEC also took administrative action against Merrill Lynch, charging that the country's largest brokerage had passed inside information about an earnings decline at Douglas Aircraft Company. The way I protected myself against any charges about privileged facts and figures was to make sure that buyers and sellers had the same research from me. And I got some of my information in ways that could hardly be claimed proprietary. One time, while vacationing in Puerto Rico, I passed the first supermarket ever built there. I gave up a day at the beach to meet with the management and then recommended the stock, which worked out beautifully. When I heard rumors about a new development at Kodak, I stopped in at two camera stores on Wall Street and asked the salesmen, "What do you think?" One told me that the company was planning to introduce a drastically different model in two or three months. He let me have one of the cameras, and I was fascinated because it was so easy to use—a no-brainer. I took it to a Christmas party, and it caused quite a stir among the other guests. When I saw that it was a hit, I visited the company's operations in Rochester, New York. The numbers made sense: The stock was priced without reflecting any new possible developments, so I recommended it. The Kodak treasurer asked how I'd heard about the breakthrough. "From one of your customers," I replied. That camera was an Instamatic. By 1970, 50 million had been produced.

2

THE LADY TAKES A SEAT

A risk-reward ratio is important, but so is an aggravation-satisfaction ratio.

In 1965, one year after Title VII of the Civil Rights Act prohibited job discrimination on the basis of sex, race, color, religion or national origin, a *Harvard Business Review* study about top-level executives noted: "In the case of both Negroes and women, the barriers are so great that there is scarcely anything to study."

That glass ceiling was just inches above my head. I was earning more than a quarter of a million dollars a year and was worth three times that, but I felt confined. As the partner of a small brokerage, I couldn't participate in the financing of a deal because my firm didn't have the capital or expertise or outreach. I had brought lucrative business to my Wall Street employers, business that I could possibly do myself. I realized that when I found attractive financing or a possible merger or acquisition, I would continue having to take it to a bigger firm. Some were offering me jobs, but I knew that the opportunities were limited. None of them had women partners, and none offered me commissions, just straight salary.

The used Studebaker that I'd driven to New York in 1954 had long since been consigned to the junk heap, but it still served as inspiration: as the car got older, the driver's side door would stick, and when talking to it didn't help, I just had to resort to kicking it. That became a metaphor for life: When you hit a closed door and it doesn't budge, just rear back and kick it in—but hold it open so others can follow you.

In spring 1967, I was lamenting my situation to my client Gerry Tsai. A maverick moneyman, he'd increased the value of Fidelity Capital Fund 40 percent two years before and had just started his own Manhattan Fund.

One afternoon, as he was walking me to my car after lunch, I asked Gerry, "What large firm can I go to and get credit for the business I'm doing?"

"Don't be ridiculous," he answered bluntly. "There's *nowhere* you can go. Buy a seat on the Stock Exchange and work for yourself."

"Don't *you* be ridiculous," I said. "There are no women on the Exchange."

"I don't think there's a law against it," he said. Gerry pointed out that many people knew the work I did and that this was the only way to get the kind of return on my productivity that I wanted. I knew he meant it and knew it was an indication of his respect, but frankly, I thought he had gone off the deep end.

That night I took home the constitution of the Stock Exchange, read it line by line and realized he was right. Theoretically, anyone who met the NYSE's standard regulations and requirements could buy a seat, as long as the board of governors

---

When you hit a closed door and it doesn't budge, just rear back and kick it in.

---

was convinced that the buyer intended to use it for legitimate business and had the purchase price. A candidate from a big firm such as Merrill Lynch might have been asked to prove that he generated business and earned commissions personally, rather than getting a token credit on certain accounts, but it was well known that my business was based on stocks I was researching. For rather obvious reasons, most Big Board seats were in the names of men affiliated with brokerage houses. The handful of freelancers who traded for their own accounts and "two-dollar brokers"—so called because they executed orders for other members for a $2 commission on each hundred-share lot—were colorful characters known to wage water pistol fights and douse each other with talcum powder or cheap cologne. They'd sing a chorus of the *Mickey Mouse Club* theme song on Friday afternoons, and on holidays, when much of the rest of the world had the day off, they'd clap or boo solidly for a few minutes at the opening bell. In their downtime, they'd invent irreverent nicknames for stocks based on the ticker symbols: "Zsa Zsa Gabor" for Continental Can, "Marilyn Monroe" for Welbilt Corporation or "Love 'Em and Leave 'Em" for Pittsburgh Screw and Bolt. But new restrictions on their activities had somewhat tamed these mavericks: a floor trader had to stabilize 70 percent of the trades for his own account—that is, buy when the stock was going down and sell when it was going up.

It took me six months to summon up the nerve to apply. I was earning a good salary, with a nice security blanket from a couple of great stocks in my portfolio. (If I'd kept the highly leveraged convertible bonds for Ryder Systems, the truck rental company, that I'd bought for $20,000 cash down—an acceptable legal margin at that time—they would have been worth more than $3 million five years later.) I was living in a comfortable apartment on Sutton Place, taking lovely vacations, enjoying what I was doing. Why rock the boat? I wondered if the almost guaranteed publicity of being the first woman would scare away clients who might suppose that financial transactions should be done in an atmosphere of propriety and privacy. I also wondered if clients would stick by me when they learned how much money I made. Most of the traders at the institutions where I did business were making $50,000 a year, the portfolio managers perhaps twice that, and I didn't know how they'd react when they found out my income was several times theirs.

It's hard to imagine that any man would have been troubled

by similar doubts and concerns, but, realistically, I had to consider what I was risking. A risk-reward ratio is important, but so is an aggravation-satisfaction ratio. I even went to a psychiatrist to examine my motivations. But during most of our sessions, he wanted to discuss what stocks I liked, and after perhaps a half dozen visits, he made the grand pronouncement that I wanted a challenge.

Buying a seat is a bid-and-ask situation, although the price may be way out of line—not what you'd call an orderly market. A seat was available for $445,000, plus an initiation fee of $7,515. (I wouldn't learn until later that it had belonged to a man named Edwin A. Meyer, who had died.) Seats on the American Stock Exchange were a lot cheaper, and in 1965 that exchange had admitted two women: Julia Montgomery Walsh and Phyllis Peterson. But the world financial markets were

---

A risk-reward ratio is important, but so is an aggravation-satisfaction ratio.

---

hardly embracing women. Just that past February, the bowler-hatted brokers of the London Stock Exchange had held off a prospective "petticoat invasion" and defeated a motion to admit women as members—an action that was rhetorically applauded by the NYSE's Big Board.

When I finally went in to see Secretary of the Exchange John J. Mulcahey, Jr., who handled the purchase of seats, I had a long speech memorized. It was a beauty: all about the honor and glory, the respected lineage and contemplated thrill of membership. But when the moment arrived, I couldn't remember a word of it and stood there more or less paralyzed. Finally I managed to sputter, "Can I buy a seat, or is this just a country club?"

"You're already an allied member as a partner of a member firm," he said. "We can't turn you down for nonbusiness reasons, on the basis of sex, or you could sue every member of the board of governors."

On December 7, 1967, I signed a conditional sales contract and wrote a check for $89,000—the standard deposit of 20 percent of the purchase price, part of which was supposed to cover the investigations that would be made to determine my eligibility. Proudfoot Detective Agency would do a thorough check into my background to establish my financial responsibility and character, as it did with all prospective members. The only skeleton in my closet was lying about having a college degree to get my first job. I had to sign a statement that said: "A member who shall be adjudged guilty of making on his [note the "*his*"] application for membership a material misstatement to the Exchange may be suspended or expelled as the board may determine." This would be a historic application, different from those I'd filled out to get my first and subsequent jobs. I had to tell the truth. When the NYSE sent me a copy of the announcement that would be made, I crossed out "was graduated from" and wrote "attended"; crossed out "bachelor of arts in" and wrote "studied."

My application was processed by George Lutes, who worked in the secretary's office as manager of admissions, handling the market for seats. He noticed that a two-person law firm and a two-person accounting firm represented me in my dealings with the NYSE. "Dearie," he declared, looking at these small fish, "you should be using much larger firms now." Appearing before the admissions committee was somewhat nerve-racking because I'd heard a rumor that my former partner Roland Stearns, still angry at my having left his firm, was bad-mouthing me on the floor of the Exchange and might try to block my approval. I was told by a floor governor that Roland had been advised either to come and face the admissions committee or stop complaining. Fortunately, his was not among the faces that greeted me that day. All I had to do was answer a few questions that I'd been told of in advance, all fairly straightforward:

—Please outline your business activities to date, with particular reference to the security and brokerage business. *(This was a basic résumé.)*

—Do you have any outside business connections to which you will devote your time? *(Nope.)*

—We understand that you are paying the entire purchase price of membership with your own means. Is this correct? *(Yep, with cash and a loan collateralized by stocks I owned.)*

—Are you a party to any agreement or understanding, oral or written, in regard to the membership? *(Nope.)*

—Do you agree that you will not, at any time, make any agreement whatever concerning the gratuity fund which is payable to the family of a deceased member? *(Under a little-known provision on the books, the Exchange refunded $20,000 to the heirs of all members who died. There have been times in history that the family of a dead broker might not have had burial money.)*

—Have you read the constitution of the Exchange? *(Of course. That's how I got here.)*

—Do you agree to abide by its provisions and the rules and policies of the board of governors adopted pursuant thereto in the event of your election? *(Certainly.)*

—If admitted for membership, what are your business plans?

This last question was loaded. A Big Board seat is actually the equivalent of a franchise to execute transactions on the trading floor, but the last time women had walked those venerable wooden boards was in wartime: In June 1943, Merrill Lynch assigned eighteen-year-old Helen Hanzelin to the floor as a telephone clerk. A month later, when it seemed that Miss Hanzelin and the hundreds of men subjected to the sight of her had managed to survive relatively intact, the Exchange assigned thirty-six women to the floor as quotation clerks and carrier pages. By 1945 there were dozens more employed by member firms—Wall Street's version of Rosie the Riveter—but they were replaced by returning veterans when the war ended. Another manpower shortage during the Korean War forced the Exchange to employ female pages and clerks again. That was the last time women had worked on the floor.

When I answered the question about my plans, the tension was visceral.

"I intend to do the same business but keep a larger share of commissions," I said.

"You're not going to work on the floor?" I was asked.

"No," I said, "I couldn't earn as much money on the floor as I do now." I could see the relief in their eyes—a delicate female would be protected from the fraternity atmosphere of the floor—and agreed to write a letter stating those intentions.

The name of any person applying for membership is posted in the Stock Exchange's *Weekly Bulletin,* and for two weeks people can object or forever hold their peace, as at a wedding. (Actually, they are invited to report "information pertinent to consideration by the board.") During final negotiations, but just before my application was posted, *The New York Times* announced my plans on its front page, along with a photo of me

---

You choose your battles.

---

looking uncharacteristically demure in a ruffled white blouse. When the reporter asked how I was going to use the seat, I replied that I intended to analyze companies and provide institutions with ideas on buying and selling stocks. The Exchange claimed that I had signed a letter saying I'd never go on the floor. I had never signed such a disclaimer, but I chose not to make an issue of the inaccuracy by sending the actual letter to the *Times.* You choose your battles.

With the application, I needed two sponsors who were themselves members or allied members (partners of a firm but not individual members of the Exchange). Nine of the ten men I asked to sponsor me ran screaming in the other direction, at least metaphorically. One was going to be out of town on vacation. Another said he didn't know me well enough. (It had been a minimum of five years.) One said, "Holy shit, Mickie, I won't have a friend left."

Finally I went to my client Ed Merkle at Madison Fund and said, "I need help."

"Money?" he asked.

"No, I'd like to go in with highest level of sponsorship I can." I was sitting at his desk when he called his buddy Gustave A. "Gus" Levy, the legendary senior partner of the distinguished and powerful banking firm Goldman Sachs and chairman of the NYSE Board of Governors.

"We don't want her, but we think we have to take her," said Levy, mentioning the lack of a ladies' room.

"She can pee in her pants, for all I care," retorted Merkle. "We do business with her because she treats us right. Will you speak up for her?" Levy refused, but at Merkle's request he promised at least not to speak against me.

I finally found two brave soldiers: Jim O'Brien, a partner at Salomon Brothers who had been head of the trust department at Chase, and Ken Ward, a research partner at Hayden Stone. Ward told me afterward that he was angered when asked, "What do you know about Miss Siebert's personal life?" He had sponsored other people, and that question had never been posed.

Before the application was considered complete, the NYSE had demanded that I secure a letter on bank stationery stating, "In the event that the New York Stock Exchange accepts the bid card from Muriel Siebert, the bank stands ready to loan her $300,000 of the $445,000 purchase price." This letter had never been asked of a man, and it represented a catch-22 because Morgan Guaranty Trust Co. of New York refused to lend me the money until the Exchange agreed to admit me. In mid-October I called Joe Debe, the analyst at Chase Manhattan. Some years before, Joe had told me about the bank's investment committee voting to sell National Cash Register. "It looks like I'm not going to get the seat," I said. Within the hour, I had a letter to the Exchange from William Burgoon, a Chase vice president, confirming the bank's willingness to finance my acquisition of a seat, a loan against stocks I owned. (Of course, the form letter had to be modified. It said: "We have this day made a loan to Mr. ————.") And the first day I was in business, before the market even opened, Tom Cahill, the head trader at Chase, called me with an order, saying, "We want to make sure you can

---

I believe in taking the Big Chance when it comes along. I follow my hunches, but before I act, I look at the numbers—inside out and upside down.

---

pay us the interest this month." The commission on the order I was given was what I owed Chase in interest on my loan that month, to the penny. But Eddy Schwenk, Chase's number two trader, later told me, "We had a bet going at the bank that we'd never have to make the loan."

Waiting for approval was one of the only times in my life that I couldn't sleep. A broker at my clearing firm reminded me that a woman had tried to buy a seat once before, but the NYSE hadn't taken her bid card. I kept wondering what would happen if I was turned down and how it would affect my professional relationships. Instead of being a bright driving force in the business, I could be an employee with a blemish on my record. *Or* headed back to Cleveland with my tail between my legs. I believe in taking the Big Chance when it comes along. I follow my hunches, but before I act, I look at the numbers—inside out and upside down. Before I made a bid for that seat, I knew exactly how much volume I would have to generate to meet the cost of the interest and pay my expenses. I had meaningful obligations, including the support of an aging mother, and if I couldn't keep up my income, my mother would have been permanently camping out on a sofabed in my apartment.

On December 28, 1967, the Big Board became coed: 1,365 men and me. I received a letter that said in its entirety: "Dear Miss Siebert, I take pleasure in informing you that you were this day elected a member of the New York Stock Exchange. Sincerely, James F. Swartz, Jr., Assistant Secretary." I went down to the Exchange and handed over a check for the balance of the $445,000, remembering an old proverb: "With money in your pocket, you are wise and you are handsome, and you sing well too." I went to a liquor store and bought three bottles of French champagne for the people in my office. Then I went to a Christmas party where a governor of the Stock Exchange asked me, "How many more women are there behind you?"—as if I were leading a parade. But I didn't celebrate that night. I had a quiet dinner alone in a neighborhood restaurant; I was that exhausted.

The headline writers had a field day. Long Island's *Newsday* said: NOW THE GIRLS WANT TO PLAY TOO. The United Press International story was titled: MILADY JOINS BIG BOARD. From the *Independent Record* of Helena, Montana, it was: SKIRT INVADES EXCHANGE; and from the *Salina* (Kansas) *Journal*: POWDER PUFF ON WALL STREET. The *Denison* (Texas) *Herald:* FIRST FEMME ON EXCHANGE. The *Fairbanks* (Alaska) *Daily News-*

"With money in your pocket, you are wise and you are handsome, and you sing well too."

Miner: GREEN-EYED BLONDE NAMED FIRST WOMAN ON EXCHANGE. I particularly liked the *Lansing* (Michigan) *State Journal:* WALL STREET SLIPPED A "MICKIE." But my real favorite was from the *Minneapolis Tribune:* GOD BLESS AMERICA—FIRST WOMAN JOINS NY STOCK EXCHANGE.

One article was titled EXECUTIVES IN SKIRTS. A Baltimore paper quoted the reaction of one male securities analyst to my new status: "When it comes to picking good investments, management is most important. Women spend an awful lot of time trying to manage their husbands, so they have a natural advantage." A New Jersey columnist mentioned my achievement alongside a lament about New York becoming another Gomorrah, since an appeals court had okayed homosexuals dancing closely together in public. The typos were especially amusing: My name was mangled as "Sieberg," "Diebert" and "Nickie," and the *New York Post* described me as a "shaply blond" working "hebind a high-piled desk." A New Zealand paper didn't buy the "shaply" business, reporting: "Muriel Siebert is unmarried, cannot cook, lives in the untidiest apartment on Manhattan's swank Upper East Side and admits to being at least ten pounds overweight. But she does have her good points." One article included a recipe for frozen vanilla soufflé with fresh strawberries, but not from my kitchen; it was from the "21" restaurant, where I'd hosted a party. A newspaperman from Minot, South Dakota (that citadel of sophistication), wrote: "A lady broker wants to buy a seat on the New York Stock Exchange. She's got this lovely chintz slipcover and no place to put it."

The public response was simply a reflection of the cultural zeitgeist, and was no different even in my own family. When I related the news to my mother, her initial reaction was an apprehensive "What am I going to tell my friends?" For her generation, having a trailblazing daughter was no badge of honor. Although she eventually took pride in my accomplishments, it would have been much easier to boast about grandchildren than about my crossing a good block.

All the men who were sworn in the same day got a scroll; I got a handshake. The bylaws of the Stock Exchange clearly state that all brokers must have this affidavit of membership prominently displayed; if an examiner came into my office and noticed its absence, I could be censured or fined. The oversight was a festering sore for me, and after six months of calling about it, I could only assume that somebody at the NYSE was mad enough to try to sabotage me. I happened to mention the dilemma to a man named Stan West, who worked at the Stock Exchange and held some influence on Wall Street as head of an investment group called Money Marketers of New York University. The next day I had my scroll, signed not by the incumbent Gus Levy but by the incoming chairman, Bernard J. "Bunny" Lasker. I offered West my profuse thanks but never asked how or why he had accomplished this miracle. I never received a reply from the Exchange as to why I had not been given a scroll even though I had called several times. Years later I saw Janet Levy, Gus's wife, who said Gus was so proud he had helped me. I started to tell her differently, but thought better of it.

There was all manner of concern for my delicate ears—with several articles postulating that a woman couldn't handle the rough language of Wall Street—and many comments about the absence of a ladies' room on the Stock Exchange floor. Not since I was a baby had so many people been so interested in my bathroom habits. Friends sent a collection of miniature toilets, outhouses and chamber pots. A typical comment from a Big Board member was "She's paying $445,000 for a seat, and we'll have to spend $500,000 to install a john." One day, when I'd been there about two years, a specialist in one of the companies I traded saw me heading upstairs to the bathroom and led me by the hand to the ladies' room on the floor that had been built for the girl pages during the Korean War. It had been there all along, but nobody had bothered to tell me.

The NYSE had dining facilities (called the Exchange Luncheon Club) on the seventh floor, with a cloakroom that had wooden cubbyholes for shoes. (The men who worked on the floor needed comfortable footwear but kept more appropriate oxfords for their noon respites.) For three years I never set foot in the place because I understood the irritation it would cause, and I wanted to show that I'd bought a seat for business, not for the publicity or the chance to be an oddity. But finally I decided to make that part of the Exchange coed too. I was told that female guests would be welcome if properly attired—no blue jeans or miniskirts. When I starting having lunch there, I went to the executive offices on the sixth floor for the closest ladies' room. But one day a group of women business owners called the Committee of 200 had a meeting at the Exchange, followed by lunch at the club. Several of the women were European (the Moët and Chandon families, several Ferragamos, one of the Fendis), and they were outraged that there were no facilities nearby, exclaiming that such a thing would never happen in a civilized country like France or Italy. That day I saw the chairman of the Exchange and threatened to have a Port-O-San delivered if a women's bathroom wasn't added to the club floor; by my twentieth anniversary, several of the old wooden telephone cubicles were sacrificed and a ladies' room built.

On the first business day of 1968, I set up shop in the giant old Equitable Building at 120 Broadway, in a corner of the boardroom at the brokerage firm Stern, Lauer & Co., with a memo pad that said: *"When I'm right, no one remembers. When I'm wrong, no one forgets."* My only hire was a male secretary who had worked for the head of Bache. As a registered rep, he could take orders. Being female had one immediate advantage: If my secretary was out, I answered my own phone in a sweet voice, and if I was too busy to talk, I took a message for myself. I was just Muriel Siebert, seat holder, not a partnership or a company. I couldn't add the *& Co.* until almost two years later, when I took on two partners. In those days there were NYSE laws against a one-person corporation. ("Dear Madam," wrote the secretary of the Exchange, "I am pleased to advise you that the board of governors at its meeting today approved your application for permission to form a member corporation under the name of Muriel Siebert & Co., Inc.") By then I'd realized that if I made my clients money with good recommendations, I was going to get the orders. *They* knew if they didn't give me the orders on the stock, I wasn't going to call them if I changed my research opinions.

To announce my membership, I hired an ad agency that did work for many financial firms but had just lost Merrill Lynch and placed a whole-page ad in *The Wall Street Journal* looking for clients. I was advised that my announcement should be different from all others. But I wanted to fit in, and I knew that the NYSE had to approve all member advertising. The first copy submitted for approval had a large photo of me with the caption "First Lady of the New York Stock Exchange—that's Miss Muriel Siebert." It was turned down because the chairman thought his wife was the first lady. The ad was changed to read "first lady *member.*" The copy also said I had done an "exceptional" job in both research and the handling of large blocks of stock; I was told to change the word to *excellent.* That's when I should have known I was going to be watched like a hawk.

Within a few weeks of the announcement, I received several proposals of marriage, including three from men in prison. (My first reaction was: Good, maybe *there* I can get away from telephones.) Every young woman fresh from college who wanted a job on Wall Street walked through my doors. I couldn't say I wasn't in, because when the door opened, there I was. I was deluged with mail from women unburdening themselves about the strife and strain of being female and begging for money to pay off mortgages or medical expenses. Every woman who was widowed and left money seemed to come calling, and I realized that none of them had a real knowledge of finance. I saw $500,000 portfolios of totally unsuitable stocks. Some of these people should have been in the highest-yielding safe bonds possible, but instead brokers had put them in what I called "American moose pasture"—my bowdlerization of *bullshit* in the presence of clients. It was outrageous: Women controlled the overwhelming majority of outstanding corporate stock in America, but their knowledge of finance was practically nonexistent. Kukla, Fran and Ollie, who were appearing in a series of NYSE-produced films on TV to explain the market in human (or at least puppet) terms, hadn't made much of a dent in the public's grasp of investing.

I commissioned a survey of 137 senior women's colleges and was shocked to learn of a huge education gap: Fully 85 percent of female graduates had never taken a single course in managing

money. Not one. A majority of the schools offered no instruc-
tion in how to invest personal funds or other aspects of pecu-
niary management. (We even counted home economics as a
"yes.") One college administrator replied that it was "not a
proper subject for ladies." The dean of an eastern college said,
"We do not feel that such courses have a place in a liberal arts
curriculum." A southern college president commented, "We
have not been able to afford the kind of instructor who would
make the courses meaningful." A midwestern college official
said, "Not enough students are interested in courses of this kind
to justify including them in our curriculum." It was inconceivable to me that the majority of women's colleges would be so
bound by tradition that they required, as prerequisites to gradu-
ation, the completion of courses in lab sciences, while denying
students the opportunity to learn basic concepts of managing
their own money. The institutions of higher learning in this
country seemed to have agreed that it was more important to
know how to dissect a frog than how to manage personal
finances.

Once a year, Manhattan's New School used to have a Saturday
session on investing for the public. I was head of the sponsors for
the meeting that year, and Gus Levy was the scheduled keynote
speaker. The stock market was trying to deal with more business
than it could handle, and the NYSE had to close on Wednesdays
to give the "back office" a chance to catch up with the unusually
heavy volume. Levy had to cancel his scheduled appearance
when he and the incoming chairman, Bunny Lasker, flew to
Washington to discuss with the SEC the progress that member
firms were making about Wednesday closings.

   That Saturday night I was at the bar of Le Périgord, a lovely
French restaurant in my neighborhood, waiting to be seated
with my date, when I was surprised to see Levy and Lasker with
their wives. I went over to their table and said, "Mr. Levy, you

were missed at today's meeting." Lasker, whose booming voice probably had been honed from years of work on the Stock Exchange floor, looked up at me and just blurted out, "Muriel, some of the men object to your being on the floor. Why don't you ABC your seat to a man?" *ABC* is basically a leasing agreement between a brokerage and an employee, enabling the firm to put a seat in the name of someone who will work the floor. It acquired the alphabetical moniker because the employee can: (A) keep the seat if he/she leaves but must buy another seat for an individual named by the firm; (B) sell the seat but return the proceeds to the firm; or (C) transfer the seat to another employee of the firm. In effect, Lasker was saying: Transfer your seat to a man.

There was no reaction from the wives—they must have been used to hearing Lasker talk that way. "Mr. Lasker," I replied, "the day that happens against my will, I'll hold the biggest goddamn press conference the city of New York has ever seen."

Six percent of the registered reps at that time were women. It was assumed that female brokers got their business from sleeping around. I used to deflect some propositions evenhandedly by saying, "I think I've met your wife." Once I was in Christ Cella's famous steak house and overheard two men talking.

"Did you see the block that Siebert crossed today?" asked one.

"Yeah," said the other. "But she sleeps with all the customers."

Excusing myself from my date, I walked over to their table. "Hi, I'm Mickie Siebert," I said cordially. "Don't give me the name if I haven't played the game."

Coming up in the business, I made it a point never to dress more chicly or expensively than the wives of my clients. But once I became a public figure, it was important to dress the part— none of that unisex "dress for success" nonsense with the little bowtie at the neck of a dark jacket. I wore designer pantsuits in red and purple under half a dozen different fur coats. There was a constant palaver about the color of my hair, which was said to become unruly at the end of a day. (No comment on all those men with comb-overs, who make a part somewhere around the earlobe and wrap their eleven strands of hair across their bald pates, as if this makes them look hirsute.)

My specialty was handling buy-and-sell orders in the stocks I researched and recommended to major investment funds, pension funds and banks, earning commissions from either the buyer, the seller or both. These deals put a premium on knowing a few stocks backward and forward—who owned them, who might be thinking of selling a block—and I made my money by finding new buyers when somebody wanted to sell or new sellers when somebody wanted to buy. Each morning before the market opened, I got on the phone and made the rounds, bidding or offering stock depending on the orders I had. I never tried to cover the waterfront but followed a few companies every day and tried to add one or two new stocks a year, looking for an industry where I could see good growth. Once I found a stock that suited me, selling to institutions was just like selling shoes— knowing the customer as well as the stock, getting a good fit. When you see the mounds of paperwork that must be done, you don't realize that there's great creativity involved in helping companies finance future growth and building up research staffs to advise businesses or individuals on how to invest.

That first full year in business, 1968, I was recommending the manufacturers of small aircraft—Piper, Beech and Cessna. There were 165 air taxi lines offering scheduled service, as opposed to 12 just three years before. The post office had granted $180,000 worth of airmail contracts the previous year; in 1968 the figure was up to $8 million. I knew that the more routes flown by the short-haul airlines, the larger and more expensive their planes would be, but in the meantime they needed smaller planes.

My approach to the market also involved an intuitive reading of the fear and greed that drove the moneymen. Since institutions were responsible for 50 percent of the daily trading volume, their clout grew even stronger as they grew richer and bigger. Every new wage settlement added to the size of the pension funds and the amount of money invested. And when the institutional investors were scared, they put their money in bonds or blue chips, so those stocks performed beautifully even in a sloppy market.

Selling to institutions was just like selling shoes—knowing the customer as well as the stock, getting a good fit.

Even when they started moving out of surefire stocks, they didn't go far afield; the lure of secondary growth stocks stemmed from their similarity to their big brothers and the fact that they held a proprietary position in an industry that was likely to outperform the general economy. But I tried to be ahead of the market: Once a group gained favor, it was hard to get an edge on the competition or to get a quantity of stock to place. I kept a cartoon on my desk that showed a conservatively dressed father yelling at his hippie son, "What do you mean I'm not a rebel? When everybody was saying, 'Sell, sell,' I was saying, 'Buy, buy.'"

My first year on my own, I earned close to $1 million in sales commissions and helped finance three prestigious private placements: Sun Chemical (a producer of printing inks), Seaboard World Airlines (an all-cargo company) and Ryder Systems (the first truck rental organization). The previous investment bankers for these companies were having a hard time raising money for them at the right price. Sun Chemical had been working with Goldman Sachs, Seaboard was using Loeb Rhodes, and Ryder was with Lazard Freres & Co. But it was Salomon, one of the two sponsors for my Big Board seat, that screwed me.

Ryder needed $20 million. Lazard was advising that the only way to get it was a private placement of bonds, convertible right at the market, carrying an 8 percent coupon. These would be

today's equivalent of junk bonds—low investment quality. I felt
the institutions that bought the stock through me would dump
it, and I thought Lazard was not finding the right customers. I
called the company founder, Jim Ryder, and said that I knew the
trust departments of major banks that owned the company's
common stock; they would be natural buyers. I was sure I could
get better terms and told him I wanted the deal for one week. I
sort of threatened him, saying I wouldn't be able to stop the
institutions from selling.

The first day, I made four or five calls to institutions that
owned the stock and then called Ryder back. "Can I go home
now?" I asked. "I've placed $8 million." The terms were 6¼, con-
vertible at about 15 percent over the market—an important difference. He said, "No, sell more." So I called Dudley Brown of
Lockheed, who was the outside head of the trust department of
United California Bank. He told me to call Phil Burge at the
bank—a good choice because the bank was in Ryder's bank line,
and it would be an advantage to have solid financing. Burge said
UCB would take $1.5 to $2 million.

I had no experience writing indentures, which are the terms
that control bonds, and I didn't have the capital to put on the
line. I needed a big brother. So I introduced the Ryder people to
Salomon, to which I had taken two other deals because of Jim
O'Brien, one of the sponsors in buying my seat. We did the private placement jointly, splitting the fee, and shortly thereafter
Salomon suggested that Ryder sell straight debt for the company to retire some bank debt—a move that would provide
long-term capital at a lower rate. O'Brien asked me what I
thought, and I said, "Good idea." I was told I would be in the
deal once again, the implication being that I'd be an equal partner. This was the first time that a woman-owned firm was in a
public underwriting.

But when I got the papers, my name was not next to
Salomon's as a joint manager in the top underwriting bracket
(the firm or firms that set the terms of the deal). We were in the

second tier. Everybody in *that* group was listed alphabetically, as is customary, except for me. My name was at the bottom of the list. I called Salomon and said, only half-jokingly, that if the list was going to be out of alphabetical order (the first time I had ever seen such a thing), it should be ladies first. I was informed (and not too nicely) that no firm would put its name under mine. I was deeply hurt but was in an untenable position: My customers owned almost half the stock of the company on my advice. I could not be responsible for the issue collapsing if I made a fuss and Salomon pulled out. I sent Salomon a telegram saying the listing was not acceptable, pulled out of the deal, never made a penny on it and never participated in any other business with the company. Twenty years later, Salomon still does not invite my firm into underwritings. I guess the people there have long memories. (P.S. Most of the firms that wouldn't put their names under mine are now out of business.)

In 1970 my firm was growing, with several more analysts added to the payroll, and I wanted to move uptown to a glass tower twenty-five stories above Park Avenue in the Bankers Trust Building. The office was being vacated by my old boss Davey Finkle, who had sublet the space from Leon Hess. The founder of Hess Oil and the owner of the New York Jets football team, he was buying Amerada Oil and moving to that company's headquarters. Hess had many offers for the space, so I asked friends at two or three institutions that owned Amerada Hess to put in a word for me. It worked. "I've been getting telephone calls," Hess told me. "Come in with a bid at the market, and it's yours."

Although my office had an aerial view of corporate canyons, I sat with my back to the window—I didn't have time to dream. It was more room than I needed, so I had negotiated the right to sublease. Any profit would go back to the bank, which ended up putting its holding company in the adjoining space. There was a private luncheon club called the Board Room in the building, and I thought it would be a convenient and congenial place to take clients to lunch, but this is what I was told: There were no women members. A *man* from my firm would have to join, make the reservation, walk me to the table, sign the check, then leave. I complained to the bank president, who said the club was totally independent and there was nothing he could do. Once again, it was a reality check. As one friend put it, "My dear, you paid $445,000 to join a club that was no longer in existence the day you joined it." Some years later, the Board Room went broke. I did not cry.

I had to give more and better advice, information and service than customers could get from anyone else. Many mornings, I awoke on a West Coast trip to an insistently ringing phone and a too-pert hotel operator chirping, "Good morning, Miss Siebert, it's 5:45. The temperature is 63 degrees, and room service is sending up your breakfast." I had to talk with my customers by 9:00 A.M. New York time. But I went after plenty of new business that I didn't get. One time I heard that Aristotle Onassis was trying to sell a large block of an aerospace company called Fairchild-Hiller Corp. I wrote to him, saying that I could sell it at a slightly higher price than he could get through another firm. (I believed this because I had an order to buy 9.9 percent of the

---

I had to give more and better advice, information and service than customers could get from anyone else.

---

company from the Keystone Funds.) Nothing happened. Another time I wrote to Carl B. Stokes, the mayor of Cleveland, asking to discuss the handling of the city's financial affairs. It would have been exciting to handle trades on behalf of my hometown. Again nothing happened.

I was intrigued when the comptroller of New York State announced his dissatisfaction with the performance of the state's money managers and the possibility of buying a Stock

Exchange seat to execute the state's own trades. I thought it was crazy and irresponsible: every state in the country, and possibly cities too, could buy seats, which would be a big loss of business

There's no shame in getting shot down.

to the Street. Since the NYSE and many of the individual members and firms made their homes in New York, the state was one of the prime beneficiaries of the industry's profitability. Undoubtedly, if the state's portfolio had performed well, commissions would be considered incidental. If the money managers were not satisfactory, then the state should switch money managers. And why should I be competing with the state on executing orders? I was already paying taxes to the state. I wrote the comptroller a letter that began, "Why bite the hand that feeds you?" and asked for the names of the state's financial advisors and the amounts of commissions paid to any brokerages running the state's money over the past ten years. Of course, I was hoping that my outrage would get him thinking and might get me a chance at doing business. I received the list of names but not the money figures, and once again, nothing happened. But there's no shame in getting shot down.

As a courtesy to the owner of a seat, the Big Board had agreed that I could participate in an occasional cross on the floor of the Exchange, under the supervision of one of the partners at my clearing firm, without taking the customary "floor test." No woman had ever done a transaction on the floor of the Stock Exchange. By 1969 it was high time.

My motivation was more economic than historic. When I joined the Exchange, floor brokerage rates were 10 to 15 percent of the total commissions. Now we had to pay a minimum fee per share for floor brokerage of transactions and a minimum clearing fee that covered billing, holding of securities for customers and other elements of the "back office." Commissions were the same per share whether the trade was one hundred shares or one million. Volume discount was implemented on the revenue side (commissions) but not on the expense side (floor brokerage and clearing), meaning that on large blocks of low-priced stocks, I paid up to 65 percent of my commissions for floor and clearing. All that money going into somebody else's pocket. If I did my own floor brokerage on the larger transactions, especially when I crossed the block, I'd hold on to that money, and the charges would be half, or 32.5 percent. I wanted my first floor trade to be a big one, so I waited for the opportunity.

On October 18, I was heading up Manhattan's East River Drive in a rented limousine on my way to Connecticut for the funeral of John C. Emery, Sr. The business of air freight forwarding did not exist until he founded Emery Air Freight in 1946, and the firm was one of first stocks I had researched because of my belief in the potential of an industry that combined two prime technological developments of our time: jet aircraft provided speed plus capacity, while computers could tell freight companies the exact status of their inventories at a given moment. Emery himself was a class act, a man who never lost his humility and warmth. Among other good works, he started an educational foundation for the sons and daughters of employees. A colleague once said that he exuded the quality of being "a completely clean man." He treated me like a person when I was little more than a trainee and gave me such honest information that I felt obligated to live up to the trust he had in me. Attending the memorial service was a show of respect for a man whose vision and humanity I admired.

Mary Welton was one of the top traders at the Massachusetts Investors Trust, the country's very first mutual fund and still one of the largest. MIT owned a large block of Servomation Corp., a food service and vending machine company that I had researched and actively traded for institutional accounts. I regularly called her office, telling her assistant, "I don't want to bore you, and don't pull Mary off the phone, but if she's going to sell Servomation, I can place it." This one morning, she called me. The limo had some kind of two-way radio, and I remember thinking it was lucky that I wasn't driving my own car, because there would have been no way for my secretary to reach me. I got the message: "Come back to New York, and it's good." I badly wanted to pay my respects to Mr. Emery. But I'd been waiting for a big block like this to be my historic first on the floor. What to do? I decided that, as a businessman, Mr. Emery would have approved, saying, "Mickie, go do your business." The limo turned around and sped downtown to the Stock Exchange.

It was only mildly bothersome that I had to be accompanied by a floor broker and wear the gold-trimmed trainee badge, hastily printed for me, which puts a specialist on notice that he's dealing with a novice. Anybody can break the trade by upping the bid so it equals the offer, which is what one of the floor traders did; but then he leaned over and kissed me, letting me know it was a joke. I crossed 212,400 shares, slicing off a bit of my $60,000 profit for the specialist. It was one of the largest blocks that traded on the floor that day. (*The New York Times* would report the occasion, describing the two-inch black alligator heels I had worn on the floor.) Afterward, there was a helicopter waiting for me at the foot of Wall Street, my office having secured landing rights in Connecticut, and I made the tail end of the memorial service.

But history, schmistory. So many people objected to my being there without passing the floor test that I had to spend thirty days down at the Exchange as a trainee, with my little badge and a senior broker by my side: C. Peabody "Peabo" Mohan, a floor partner at Stern, Lauer, where I cleared. There were rules about the way orders should be handled, and some of the practices were not written down anywhere. Let's say that there were two buyers for a stock, both willing to pay the best offering price. Sometimes a decision would be made with the toss of a coin. Sometimes the two parties would split it. If I had a big sell order and someone else had a smaller one, I might let one of the buyers take the little piece just to get him out of the way.

John Coleman was a floor specialist known as the Dean of Wall Street. The son of an Irish cop, he rose through the ranks, eventually to become chairman of the NYSE. When I'd bought the seat, I'd asked his brother Bill, a floor broker, to sponsor me, but John had forbidden it. (The day I put in my bid card, Bill called me at home. "My brother asked if you were at least good-looking," he reported. "I said, 'Nah, she's a dog.' So he asked, 'Does she have money?' I said, 'Nah, she's buying it with bananas.'") But when I went down to pass the floor test, John Coleman spent half an hour in the middle of the floor talking to me. That was his way of saying, "She's here, and I approve."

After I'd passed the test, I have to admit that I sometimes enjoyed flaunting my presence. Floor brokers generally had two order pads for making notations and recording executed orders that were handed to a clerk; in the days before electronic transmissions, confirmations were made from those slips of paper. The pads were a standard white with black printing for a purchase and red for a sale. I ordered pink pads—in retrospect, a shade too cute.

For ten years—with the exception of a few months—the New York Stock Exchange consisted of 1,365 men and me. I was delightfully outnumbered. It wasn't until May 1970 that I was joined by a second woman, Jane R. Larkin, a partner in the venture consultancy Hirsch & Co. Big Board membership had dropped to the relative bargain price of $180,000 largely because of gloomy market conditions and dismal earnings. I sent Jane a nicely framed announcement of her membership and received a gracious thank-you, but I never got a chance to know her: Two months later, she lost her membership when Hirsch merged with two other companies and her seat was transferred to a man. In February 1970 a former professional football player named Joseph Louis Searles III became the first black member of the Big Board, an event that was heralded in *The New York Times* under the headline NEGRO PROPOSED FOR

A SEAT ON EXCHANGE. It was not an auspicious moment for such an undertaking, and before the year was out, he had lost his entire personal stake, resigned his seat and left Wall Street.

Actually, there was a one-hour period in late 1972 when the NYSE was again exclusively male: I sold my seat. And bought another. Several people who were joining Siebert & Co. wanted to use the seat, and since the price had dropped from $445,000 to $180,000, I got a $270,000 tax loss, exempt from the "wash sale rule": Generally, under today's IRS rulings, if you want to take a loss and buy back the same securities, you have to do it in one of two ways. Let's say your Lucent Technologies stock is way down. You can sell it and take your loss, but you can't buy it back for thirty days. If the market goes up 10 percent in that time, you've got an additional loss when you buy it back. Or you can "double up": If you have 200 shares, you can buy another 200 and hold 400 shares for thirty days; then you can sell the original 200 and take your loss. But the IRS decreed that a Stock Exchange seat is like any other asset: You can sell a truck and buy another that day; the same with a Big Board seat.

The NYSE required all seats to be in the name of an individual, so I signed a standard agreement whereby I would hold the seat but the firm would own it. My sponsor this time was none other than John Coleman. In one of life's little ironies, he had become a valued friend. When I brought him the papers, he said, "Where do I sign?" I asked if he didn't want to look them over first, and he said simply, "I know you." Because of this bit of paperwork, I have a second letter, almost five years to the day after the first, saying: "Dear Miss Siebert: I take pleasure in informing you that you were this day elected a member of the New York Stock Exchange." A few years later, I requested a letter from the Big Board verifying the purchase of that seat. The response was addressed to the attention of Muriel F. Siebert. The salutation was: "Gentlemen."

3

SAVING LOCKHEED

You make money by taking a stand and being right.

I am somewhat plump, smart, happy and lucky. All but the first have stood me in good stead. The serendipity of getting airlines when I first arrived on Wall Street and finding that the assignment suited me paid off handsomely. In such a male-dominated industry, I got to be a familiar face. I was the first woman member of the Wings Club, whose members were the executives of airlines and aerospace companies. Their monthly lunches presented the leading industry speakers. And I was the first securities analyst to attend the biennial aviation show at Le Bourget Airport outside Paris. For some reason, nobody else who covered the industry had ever thought of going. I was wildly enthusiastic about the new commercial jumbo jets; once passengers saw the interior of those wide, comfortable planes, they wouldn't want to be stuffed into smaller aircraft. But I was wary of the high costs of training airline personnel to operate these behemoths, which would cut into the cost-saving features of the big planes. The Boeing 747 pilots would come from the ranks of the 727 pilots, who would in turn be upgraded from the 707. That meant three training programs, not one.

I studied Lockheed so thoroughly and handled so much of its stock that Dudley E. Brown, the company's vice president for finance, would tell institutional investors, "Call Mickie Siebert—she knows more about us than anyone else." Based in Los Angeles and worth more than $2 billion, Lockheed was on the cutting edge of design and technology. The head of engineering research and development was a rumpled genius named Clarence "Kelly" Johnson, whom nobody was allowed to bother at his lab, called Skunk Works. (Once, after I'd enjoyed dinner with Brown and Johnson at the Plaza Hotel in New York, they announced their intention of "walking Mickie home." This consisted of stopping for a drink at the first bar on the left and the first bar on the right of every block. Luckily for me, I lived just a few blocks away.) Under Johnson's aegis, the company had developed Deep Quest, a submarine that could submerge lower in water and withstand more pressure than any other, and the SR-71 supersonic military spy plane. The U.S. government wanted a supersonic passenger plane, and Lockheed submitted a design made of titanium that would have traveled three times the speed of sound, or mach 3, with a variable "swing-wing" that retracted when the plane was aloft. But Boeing got the contract on an SST (supersonic transport) with a fixed-wing design. Then, while still in the planning stages, it tried to switch to a variable-wing. The government decided not to proceed, so the United States never got a passenger supersonic like the French- and British-designed Concorde, which is made of aluminum, goes only mach 2.2 and holds a fraction of the passengers that ours would have accommodated.

Lockheed was consistently one of the biggest defense/space contractors, and it had won two plums: the army's AH-56A Cheyenne helicopter and the air force's C-5A Galaxy large cargo plane. But things soured when both projects ran into cost overruns, just around the time that Congress was increasingly looking to cut back on military spending. Research and development for the Cheyenne came to more than double the original estimate of $77.5 million, and the cost per unit climbed from $992,000 to $2.2 million; Lockheed was demanding a price adjustment because of the army's delay in exercising its production option.

I practically felt like a midwife for the monster C-5A, having followed it since its conception. After *Look* magazine published a photograph of me standing on its wing, I got a letter from Carl M. Cleveland, Boeing's director of public relations, good-naturedly chastising me: "Women are fickle. You're breaking my heart. Let me tell you something. The C-5A, like the Exchange, doesn't have a ladies' room either. *Our* new 747 has twelve." But the original estimate of $3.4 billion for 120 C-5As climbed to $4.3 billion. Some of it was related to inflation and the skyrocketing prices of subcontractors due to the demands of the Vietnam War; some was due to technical problems, such as the redesign of the wing and the need to overcome excess weight. Lockheed officials argued that the 25 percent increase over the original estimate was not excessive, citing a Harvard Business School report that the cost of a dozen major defense systems developed in the 1950s had exceeded their estimated costs by an average of 220 percent. A more philosophical viewpoint was expressed by Lockheed's president, A. Carl Kotchian, who argued, "If you don't have problems with a new aircraft or missile, it means you haven't taken a big enough step forward."

Most procurement contracts on new technology are "cost-plus"—cost plus a fixed fee. But a few years earlier Defense Secretary Robert S. McNamara had changed the rules, and now companies were required to bid a single fixed sum for overall costs to develop, test and produce the aircraft. The problems with the military contracts had jeopardized Lockheed's intended expansion into commercial markets with the development of the L-1011 airbus. Start-up costs were draining the company's coffers, and it was widely assumed that the boards of directors of commercial airlines might reconsider giving orders to a company in financial straits, in all likelihood giving the business instead to McDonnell Douglas and its competitive DC-10. By 1971 Lockheed was going broke, despite its advanced technology.

All the aviation companies had little "chalets" at Le Bourget. I was standing on the balcony of Lockheed's cabin talking about the terrible far-reaching domino effect of a Lockheed bankruptcy: There were several hundred subcontractors, most of which were not due to receive any payments until Lockheed started making deliveries on the L-1011s, and the delays were causing a cash squeeze at many of these small, medium and large companies. Several major airlines had made substantial progress payments toward their airbus orders, and they were in no shape to ante up extra money to keep the project alive—the previous year, TWA had run $64 million in the red.

When I got back to the States, I got a call from Lockheed's two congressional lobbyists: Larry Merthan, a Democrat, and Robert Keith Gray, a Republican, both vice presidents at the Hill & Knowlton public relations firm in Washington, D.C. They had heard about my conversation in Paris and asked if I would testify before Congress on behalf of the company. I said yes. But the next day I changed my mind. I had a small brokerage, and while I knew what I was talking about, there was no way I could stand up against the research capabilities of larger firms. I would have alienated other aviation firms that wanted Lockheed to go broke. Whoever made engines for the competing planes would have had a dozen people working around the clock and feeding the congressmen questions designed to discredit me. If the situation were reversed, I'd do the same. Would I care if some of my competitors went out of business? I'd be thrilled. But if my reputation was damaged, institutions would stop giving me orders, and aviation stocks were a big piece of my business. I was in expensive office space and would have to fold tent.

Instead, we agreed that I would write a letter to Senator John J. Sparkman, chairman of the Senate Committee on Banking, Housing and Urban Affairs, explaining my beliefs and making myself available to talk with individual senators. If Lockheed went bankrupt, the adverse effects on the industry would be incalculable, with broad ramifications for our country's position in world aviation and the future of both commercial and military programs. In the past, these programs had been financed largely by corporate long-term debt and bank loans. But some of the newer programs involved more investment than the total net worth of the corporations doing research and development, inventory buildup and prototype testing. The risk-reward ratio—the tool that all lending officers rely on to make decisions—would preclude knowledgeable institutional investors from buying debt securities unless there was a guarantee that the principal would be repaid or an interest rate considerably above the prime rate to compensate for the risk. Higher interest rates would increase the price of any program and make America's commercial products less competitive than foreign ones. Anybody attending the past several international air shows in Paris would realize that our position in worldwide aviation was already being eroded. I argued that if Lockheed went bankrupt and its debt holders received nothing, or just a small portion of their investments, other aviation companies would find it impossible to finance future large projects without a government guaranty. TWA, Eastern Airlines and Delta Airlines had already invested, respectively, $110 million, $73 million and $30 million in the L-1011; their losses would be crippling if Lockheed went under—the proverbial ripples in a pond.

It was a five-page letter that I wrote to Senator Sparkman, an Alabama Democrat. And I spoke, both on the phone and in person, with several senators lined up by the lobbyists, who later told me that my efforts had swung the vote for the government to give Lockheed a guarantee, keeping the company afloat. I asked that the letter be included in the printed volume of the hearings but was informed that it had arrived too late. The next time I saw Merthan, he admitted that he'd been afraid to call me because my phone might be tapped. Reg Kearton, who ran Lockheed Missile and Space, asked me, "Why did you stick your neck out like that when you weren't even paid?" I didn't think in terms of money. It was the right thing to do. You make money by taking a stand and being right.

It was wonderful to see how Lockheed and the C-5A stole

the thunder at the next Paris Air Show—nobody could believe that a box that big would fly. But the aviation industry in the United States was in a backwater. Most of the world's attention was focused on the Soviet Tupelov Tu-144 supersonic planes (called STOL for short-takeoff-and-landing) and the British-French SST (not yet called Concorde). I was looking for a little more U.S. action in aerospace. I wanted to look in on Boeing, but the company hadn't allowed an analyst to cross its portals in more than a year. I thought it stunk that a publicly owned company would hold industry analysts at bay until the officials had something favorable to say, and I wrote a hot-blooded letter about it to Boeing's chairman, William Allen. It was so hot that I didn't mail it.

I was at the Beverly Hills Hotel when I heard that James Smith McDonnell, chairman of McDonnell Douglas Corporation, wanted to sell a large block of Beech Aircraft. As a young man, this aviation pioneer now known as Old Man Mac had traded his winter coat money for his first ride in a rickety biplane, and

You make money by taking a stand and being right.

he had started his first company to build the Doodlebug, a single-engine plane with spectacular takeoff and landing capabilities but also spectacularly bad timing—built for an international aircraft competition whose deadline was October 1929. The plane itself crashed soon after the stock market did, during a test flight, when McDonnell rode it to the ground and suffered severe damage to his back. (He said he was too much of a Scotsman to use the parachute.) He continued to fly the repaired Doodlebug in air shows around the country, hoping to sell personal airplanes to America the way Henry Ford sold cars, but the Great Depression eliminated the private market for planes, and nobody could afford to buy it. In 1931, McDonnell sold the Doodlebug to the National Advisory Committee for Aeronautics, which would become NASA, for use as a test plane. In 1939, he formed the corporation that would become the leading producer of jet fighters and would build the first spacecraft to carry an American into orbit. A 1967 merger with the Douglas Aircraft Company created the behemoth McDonnell Douglas.

Over the years, I had heard rumors that McDonnell owned a large block of Beech and wanted to own the company, but after buying Douglas, he realized that absorbing both at one time was too ambitious. When I heard about his plans to sell his shares of Beech, I called and said that I had placed a large amount of that stock, having represented both sides of the trade in a $16 million deal that had taken place by phone in two hours.

"How much can you take?" he asked.

"I'll take one hundred thousand shares," I said.

"I have more," he said.

I called him back an hour later. "I'll take two hundred thousand," I said. "But I need to know the total."

"I have more than two hundred thousand," he said.

"I'll take all of your stock or nothing," I said, and he agreed. I lined up the buyers and crossed the stock.

Beech was run by Olive Ann Beech, the widow of the founder, Walter Beech. I called her to say, "You're going to see a big block of your stock trade on the New York Stock Exchange. It's McDonnell's stock going to the following institutions." (It was a courtesy call *and* almost an insurance policy that the next time I wanted to see her, my entrée would be greased and immediate.) A couple of days later, after the block traded, Mrs. Beech called me. "You ought to use your commission to buy an airplane," she suggested. I had no such intention, but I'd been thinking of taking flying lessons. So I called Hayden Wehren, who covered Wall Street for Beech, to ask if he knew a good flight instructor for a beginner.

"Would you mind taking lessons from a black man?" he asked.

"A black man, no," I said. "A blind man, yes."

After several months of lessons at Westchester Airport, my instructor couldn't understand why I was having so much trouble judging distance to land the plane. He stood six feet four inches tall; I was only five foot three, and I couldn't see over the hood. "Bring a pillow," I was told. From that day on, I had no problem.

I never bought a plane, but I did acquire some other nice wheels. Mercedes-Benz had introduced the 350SL sports car in Europe, but there was a two-year waiting period for one in the U.S. Larry Merthan, the Lockheed lobbyist, happened to have dated a woman who was now married to the head of Mercedes. I called Larry and said, "I think the first woman member of the Stock Exchange should have the first 350SL that comes into this country." One day I received a phone call from the president of Mercedes North America, a German man with little sense of humor.

"The first car here will be on display in the New York showroom," he said, "and you can have it. It's silver."

I had wanted white. "What color silver?" I asked.

"Rolls-Royce silver."

"Is it proper for a Mercedes to be Rolls-Royce silver?"

"You will take it, yes?" he said.

"I will take it, yes," I answered.

I still have the car. I've gone to trade it in several times but always changed my mind. It meant so much to me. I guess it meant arriving—in style.

4

I CAN GET IT FOR YOU DISCOUNT

Any significant change in business is an opportunity for new business.

When I first got into the business, there were four distinctly different kinds of stockbrokers. The big guns—Merrill Lynch, Paine Webber, Kidder Peabody, Smith Barney—were "supermarkets" offering a plethora of financial products, from stocks and bonds to commodities and tax advice. There were hundreds of "corner grocers"—small investment firms, like the kind where I worked early in my career. Investment bankers such as Morgan Stanley or Goldman Sachs raised money for corporations and catered to an upscale clientele, offering prestige along with advice. Some specialty houses carved out particular niches, like Lebenthal & Co. for tax-free bonds. But despite differences in size and scope, by law brokers had to charge the same commission rates, based purely on the number of shares and the price of a stock. The charge to an investor was approximately 1 percent of the dollar value of the transaction, whether the trade was for 100 shares or 10,000, even though the larger trade certainly didn't cost 100 times more than the smaller one. The only exception was the handful of brokerages around the country known as the "third market," offering over-the-counter trades at reduced rates. These firms were not members of the Stock Exchange and not subject to its regulations, but what they did was considered heresy. Apart from these few renegades, fixed trading commissions had prevailed on the Big Board for almost two hundred years, from the signing of the Buttonwood Agreement.

The 1970s was the decade of change. On April 1, 1971 (April Fool!), the SEC permitted negotiation of all commissions on that part of an order over $500,000. About a year later, this figure was lowered to affect trades upward of $300,000. But it still wasn't fair. There was too much money being made on crossing blocks of stock. I could cross 25,000 shares (not such a big block) and make more money than my father made standing on his feet for a year as a dentist. But the move toward negotiated rates wasn't spurred so much by the desire to help the public, many of whom no doubt believed that the current means of paying for the purchase and sale of securities was unfair. It was impelled by institutions threatening to take their business off the Board.

The old fixed-rate schedule was clearly an antitrust violation, but many brokers argued that such an industry umbrella was vital. I had major concerns about the encroachment of competition for the small investor, whose commissions were already significantly higher per share for large trades than those for big institutions. The liquidity of the market was jeopardized because the little guy would be squeezed out. This was before the Internet, and information on companies was not easy to come by. Small investors were dependent on their brokers for advice. Big institutional investors could strike hard bargains with their brokers, but who would benefit? Say that an insurance company was the client: Were the savings passed on to individual policyholders? Or if the savings went toward higher salaries for the money manager who scored the coup, did that precipitate better performance of the portfolio and consequently more money for individuals?

By the mid-'70s, even bigger changes were in the works. One was ERISA: the Employee Retirement Income Security Act of 1974 (commonly dubbed Everything Ridiculous Invented Since Adam). This federal law established legal guidelines for private pension plan administration, and it stipulated that any fiduciary running money for people had to get the best execution of an

order at the lowest cost. Then, on May 1, 1975, the SEC instituted fully negotiated brokerage rates for trading listed securities. This single "May Day" ruling mandated fully negotiated
brokerage commissions and changed the face of the investment
business. Fixed stock commissions ended; price joined service as
a selling point. If one law had passed without the other, it would
have been a nonevent. But the two together meant that my current business was finished: How would clients justify paying me
anything other than the lowest rates? They might value my
research, but that was a commodity they could not quantify.

Whenever there is a significant change in business, there must
be an opportunity for new business to be created. The new business would come in executing orders, and indeed the new firms
were quickly known as "execution-only"—an ominous-sounding
moniker that jibed perfectly with the dour predictions about
what this meant for the research industry. Discounters were
ridiculed as "pipe-rack companies," shoestring operations, under-
financed, with order clerks (who were fully licensed but not commissioned) rather than experienced registered brokers executing

> **Whenever there is a significant change in
> business, there must be an opportunity
> for new business to be created.**

orders. It was no-frills investing: no stock analysis, no research,
no trading advice. There were accusations of inaccurate monthly
statements, no back-office follow-through, inferior clearing
firms, no direct access to floor people to ensure exact and prompt
transactions, and insufficient insurance protection. Some firms
carried only the minimum amount required by the Securities Investor Protection Corporation.

In fact, the advent of discounting constituted perfect timing
after the string of economic collapses that plagued Wall Street
from 1970 through 1975, when there was a mass exodus of
almost six million people from the stock market, most of them

under the age of forty-five. Small investors had gone through frustrating and costly experiences; many had lost faith in the market and were disillusioned with their broker's performance. (One time a woman rushed up to me in the supermarket and demanded, "What have you done to my AT&T?") Some reentered the marketplace with new attitudes and a new sophistication, willing to make their own investment decisions; others were unhappy to be losing capital while paying exorbitant commissions for that privilege and felt they could do no worse at a cut-rate price. But despite the furor from the halls of convention, discounting did not harbinger the demise of traditional brokers. Customers were confronted with a huge variety of financial products—money market funds, convertible securities, option trading—and some would always be too harried to do their own research or make their own decisions. Such people don't have the time, inclination or motivation to do their own investment thinking. They'd still need guidance and hand-holding.

Long before May Day, everybody on Wall Street knew that many research firms were going to be phased out or merged out of the brokerage business because, in the past, researchers had been paid commissions by financial institutions. The new laws would change everything. It took me a year and a half to shrink my business, cut the research department and pare the staff from eight to four. Sometimes shrinking is better than growing. After the long shakeout in the industry, almost fifty brokerage houses had shut down or merged with others. To promote my business, I had yo-yos made up with my name printed on them. (I was yo-yo champion at the Doan Elementary School in Cleveland, and I

Sometimes shrinking is better than growing.

---

can still do a mean cat's cradle and loop-the-loop.) Some men would play with them on the floor of the Exchange during a market break. It was a good metaphor for the stock market: up and down, up and down, up and down.

I'd been able to keep my firm going, but an estimated 50 percent drop in business wouldn't even touch what had happened,
and what happened on Wall Street hit people's egos as much as
their pocketbooks. Almost four thousand part-time brokers
left the business, and some of the survivors turned to driving
cabs and tending bar. (In an effort to keep up with the times,
the NYSE eased its rule against moonlighting, although it still
drew the line at casino dealing.) Nobody was holding any
telethons for me—I could still take clients to lunch and come
home to my apartment on the East River—but I used to love to
go to work, and now it was just labor. I felt as if somebody had
stolen my lollipop.

The British statesman David Lloyd George said: Don't be
afraid to take a big step—you can't cross a chasm in two small
jumps. I became a discount broker at the opening bell on May 1,
1975, and was on the front page of *The Wall Street Journal* the
next day. At first we offered our service to institutional clients,
which constituted almost all of the business. Our brokers were
all registered reps of the NYSE, where all orders were received
and executed. We had direct access to all the major exchanges,
including direct lines to members on the floor. We performed all

---

**Don't be afraid to take a big step—you can't
cross a chasm in two small jumps.**

---

the major functions of traditional full-service brokers, except
advising clients what or when to buy or sell. We gave quotes,
market information and status reports on clients' accounts. Discounters don't have the high overhead of research teams, elabo-
rate offices and publications—savings that we passed on to the
customers. We avoided the "let's get big fast" syndrome by keeping the business in New York—no branches.

I had been operating out of an office at Bear Stearns, my longtime clearinghouse. When I informed the firm of my new business plan, I offered to pay the same absolute dollars for clearing

and floor brokerage that I had been paying under the fixed-rate schedule. An article in *Institutional Investor* alleged that I was promoting my clearing relationship, promising clients "Bear Stearns executions at Muriel Siebert prices." Interestingly, the writer refused to name the "confidential sources" for this inaccurate insinuation. But Alan C. "Ace" Greenberg, a principal of the firm (and later its chairman of the board and CEO), told me that it wouldn't be good business practice to process my orders at a discount. I received formal notice that our agreement would be terminated in sixty days. While still looking around for another affiliation, I was informed by a long time institutional client that Bear Stearns was passing my orders on to two-dollar brokers. When I requested at least the right to use a two-dollar broker of my own choosing, I was told it would tie up the company's booths, wires and floor clerks.

It seemed there was no room for me at several inns. Since Bear Stearns no longer wanted to clear my trades, I decided to clear through an old-line bond firm called Aisel. But the morning that I was supposed to sign the standard clearing contract, one of the partners there called and said, "Please don't come in—and don't take it personally." Eventually, I found a clearing firm in Becker Securities and moved to 55 Broad Street. Some people called it the Goldman Sachs building. I thought of it as the Siebert building. I was on a higher floor.

Almost immediately, a rumor began circulating around the Street that my firm was going under, despite the fact that audits showed us to be financially sound and profitable. A rumor like that had to be planted, and I swore that if I ever found out who was behind it, I'd bring the guy up on charges. But I was hardly singled out. There was a pervasive impression that the discounters would wither and die—which would have been just fine with the big guns who were appalled by the drastic price-cutting and called us vultures. Quick & Reilly was disparaged as "Quick & Dirty." Charles Schwab, not yet a member of the NYSE, was operating out of a two-room office and offering free Brownie

cameras to attract customers. There was a prevailing feeling that
we belonged to the scrappy, seamy underbelly of the profession.
One institutional trader asked me, "What are you doing in a
shyster business?" (It wouldn't have bothered me so much,
except that I was paying for his lunch at the time.)

The image problem was often the result of an assumption
that any firm to go the discount route did so only because of a
shaky capital position, rather than seizing the zeitgeist, and it
was fueled by occasional insidious reports of shoddy or faulty
executions. One major brokerage house presented its institutional clients with Lucite blocks containing pieces of ticker tape
that showed a large trade done at 3¾ points above the last sale. A
message embedded in the block noted: "This transaction was
handled by a new form of organization created to service institutions post–May 1, 1975, known as a 'discount boutique.'" It
was as if Ford Motor Company had sent little pieces of
chopped-up tires and steering wheels embedded in Lucite to its
car buyers, noting that the damaged goods represented a new
type of automobile known as a Hyundai.

Six months after May Day, the brokerage of Delafield Co.
became the first discounting casualty, and there was enough evidence of hostile activity by some major firms and institutions
that the Justice Department announced a full-scale investigation
about antitrust violations and restraint-of-trade tactics. The
possible charges included: setting an artificial floor on rates by
refusing to deal with discounters; changing or terminating clearing arrangements because of a discounter's low rates; discriminatory treatment against discounters by specialists and other
floor brokers; and predatory pricing below actual costs to drive
smaller firms out of business.

Some people in the securities industry had fatuously labeled
May Day a "nonevent." Edward I. O'Brien, president of the
Securities Industry Association, predicted that there would be
less negotiating between brokers and clients than anticipated,
and indeed, dozens of brokers were relieved to discover that

many retail customers didn't even ask what they were paying in commissions, let alone try to haggle. Some institutional clients switched their most easily executed orders—say, 500 shares of IBM—to discounters. But they kept their more difficult transactions, requiring wide institutional connections and special floor expertise, with their old-line brokerages (arguing that they never should have paid higher commissions for the "no-brainer" trades all along). It became quite clear, as one financial wag put it, that minimizing May Day as no great shakes was akin to depicting the Watergate break-in as a "third-rate burglary attempt."

Rate competition was profound and swift, first heated and then brutal. What one trader described as the "threshold of pain" was constantly revised downward as major financial clients began bargaining ferociously for deep concessions, and the argument that cheap rates meant inept executions became less and less tenable as even the most conservative brokerage houses were bidding for their business. Wall Street had to learn to live with the kind of price competition championed by almost any other industry and considered "the American way." New guidelines at the good, gray Goldman Sachs called for the elimination of an 8 percent commission rate increase that had been imposed the previous year to help offset the low trading volume, and other companies soon began discussing their own rates as "roughly the same as Goldman Sachs'," or "very close to Goldman Sachs'," or "up and down from Goldman Sachs'." Major firms replaced boutiques as the most aggressive price competitors. White, Weld & Co. began handing out T-shirts to institutional clients and its own traders emblazoned with a catchphrase from John F. Kennedy's inaugural address: "Let us never negotiate out of fear, but let us never fear to negotiate." The president of Morgan Stanley flatly refused to discuss commission rates, saying, "I'd just as soon let other people talk, and we'll negotiate the best we can." But a year after May Day, the firm began an entirely separate entity called Execution Services, Inc., with its own Stock Exchange seat, to handle the discount business at prices as low as eight cents a share—much lower than most other deep discounters. This whitest of the white-shoe firms was legitimizing what Delafield had been driven out of business for doing. Only on Wall Street, it was said, could a company go belly-up for being a few months ahead of its time. You can be ahead of your time, just not *too* far ahead.

After May Day, when I announced my policy of deep discounting, I was getting looks that could kill at the Exchange Luncheon Club, particularly from floor brokers. (I showed up more often than usual just to prove that I wasn't intimidated.) But within a few months, I got some smiles and nods of recognition again from the once hostile. On occasion, a specialist even admitted, sotto voce, "Mickie, you were absolutely right, and if I'd been in your place, I'd have done the same thing." Some clearing firms that had shunned me came sniffing around again, asking if I was satisfied with Becker. "Delighted," I'd say—then I'd tell them where they could go and what they could do once they got there.

Discounting took on an actual patina of respectability when Fidelity Group, the old-line Boston-based financial services organization, added a discount brokerage to its list of services. In fewer than ten years, discounters captured about 20 percent of

---

You can be ahead of your time, just not *too* far ahead.

---

all commission dollars and 35 to 50 percent of all new retail customers entering the stock market. I never expected the major firms to come down to the boutiques' rates, and I had to fight the notion that, on an equal playing field, the customer would get more bang for his buck at a bigger firm, that eight cents spent at Paine Webber would get more than eight cents spent at Muriel Siebert. The only way to do that was to create value and convince people that their commissions meant a lot more to us, and that they wouldn't be paying for the layers and levels of employees—the salesmen, the brokers, the commission people—of a large firm. Customers got the best price *and* execution, meaning no junior order clerks handling the sale or the order.

I'd been concentrating on institutional customers ever since I started my own firm. That's where the big money was. But by 1976 I could see an opportunity in aggressively advertising to individual accounts and extending them the same cut rates. May Day had meant almost nothing to the individual investor, who continued to pay two, three or four times as much as an institution with bargaining power. The two-tiered commission structure was simply unfair to the little guy, even if he was unaware of the disparity. I had seen too many cases where the broker made more in commissions than the customer made in profit. When the SEC ruled that commissions be negotiable, it did not intend that banks and insurance companies would pay a small fraction of what John (and Jane—never forget Jane) Q. Public paid for identical transactions.

In September I held a press conference at "21" with the noted economist Eliot Janeway by my side, whom I knew from my lunches with Scarsdale Fats. I announced that I would be the first stockbroker to offer a 50 percent discount to retail customers year-round—the same kind of break that the institutions had been getting. Now all accounts would get equal treatment, no strings attached. No minimum annual commission volume, no membership fees, no restrictions about trading at off-peak hours. Year-round sale—half off!

All that a customer had to do to figure out the commission rate was to look up the rate effective prior to May 1 and cut it in half. But people didn't seem to believe it. Lots of calls came in on our WATS line asking what would be the charge to buy such and such. I'd say, "Well, the old rate was $520, so now it will be $260." And the reply on the other end would be "The dirty bastards!" I'd say, "You have to realize that we're not giving you any research or opinions," and I'd hear "I don't *want* any, lady. All they've done is cost me money."

I knew I would take some flak from the major wire houses, but I was prepared to take on Messrs. Merrill, Lynch, Pierce, Fenner, Smith, Barney, Paine, Webber, Jackson, Curtis, Hutton, Halsey, Stuart, Eastman, Dillon, Shearson, Hayden, Stone, Dean and Witter. I knew it would be called "slumming," "a step down," a far cry from the "prestige" business of dealing exclusively with "customers" made of mortar and red brick, with multimillions to invest. The big brokerage houses claimed that most individual investors needed research and investment advice, which didn't come at bargain prices. At these rates, they warned, there would be nobody watching customers' portfolios and making recommendations for timely sales or purchases.

For my part, I didn't understand why the big guys didn't at least open an execution-only desk for people who didn't want extra services. Broadscale discounting would mean more competition, a likely rate war and a radical change in the roles of registered reps and security analysts. My own staff was on salary with year-end bonuses, not commissions. (In full-service firms, about 30 to 40 percent of the customer's commission dollars went to brokers.) Some customers themselves were suspicious. One woman called and said, "Okay, now what's the catch?" But in the month following my first ad (a photo of me taking a large pair of shears to a $100 bill), I received more than two thousand

> "The only difference between 'chairwoman'
> and 'charwoman' is the letter *I*."

requests for information. We got considerable walk-in business and opened four hundred new accounts for people who were happy to stop subsidizing the influential institutions. One woman came in to buy 100 shares of the Long Island Lighting Co.; when she heard what the cut-rate commission was, she said, "I'll take two hundred." Another was so pleased to learn she would cut her costs in half that she brought us a chocolate cake. I had twenty-eight buttons on my phone, and they lit up continuously from about an hour before the opening bell of the Stock Exchange until an hour beyond closing. (People always seemed surprised when they got me. "All the lights were lit up," I'd say. "The boss *works* here.") To my four employees, I'd say: "The only difference between 'chairwoman' and 'charwoman' is the letter *I*." All of us responded to queries on quotes, wrote up orders, called them in to the clearing firm, received verbal confirmation, phoned back clients and handled applications from new investors. I had to halt advertising until I could hire more people to handle the steady flow of fresh business—a baker's dozen by the beginning of 1977.

My motives have always been pride, principle and profit. I don't know how you stay afloat and sleep at night without all three. I thought that small investors deserved a break and was willing to bet that there were opportunities in offering them that break. It paid off. No fewer than two dozen other firms

---

My motives have always been pride, principle and profit. I don't know how you stay afloat and sleep at night without all three.

---

became discounters when I did on that May Day so many ago. Mine is the only NYSE firm that started on day one and is still in business.

5

SUPERINTENDENT OF BAKING

A woman can be an S.O.B.

In the spring of 1977, I got an unexpected call from Robert J. Morgado, secretary and top aide to the Democratic governor of New York, Hugh Carey. Would I be interested in the position of superintendent of banking? "We've made a commitment to hire women," said Morgado, "and yours is the only name that keeps coming back." The governor reiterated this pledge and compliment when we met a few days later. The job was mine if I wanted it.

The timing of the offer was not brilliant. My mother, a smoker who developed blood clots, had been hospitalized for nine months while doctors tried to restore her circulation, but when one leg turned gangrenous, it was amputated. (Everybody on Wall Street smoked, but I stopped cold turkey the day I saw my mother on the surgical gurney.) That winter, she'd suffered a stroke, and the only thing she could move was the stump and one arm. Amazingly, she could still sing, and her lovely voice sometimes filled the whole corridor of the hospital. (As a young woman, she'd been offered professional opportunities, but at that time nice Jewish girls didn't go on the stage.) Her insurance coverage was exhausted, and I was supporting her at a private nursing home on the Upper East Side, but her condition had deteriorated terribly. The situation was so emotionally draining that I didn't think I could possibly spare the time and energy to gather the documentation and financial information required for the state job (including five years of personal checkbooks). Even though I'd have nothing to do with regulating the brokerage industry, I'd have to put my firm in a blind trust (the NYSE had never allowed a member to do that) and take a position that paid $47,800 a year, or about one tenth of what I was earning in the stock market. Private care for my mother, including round-the-clock nurses, had cost me $250,000 the previous year. Ironically, becoming superintendent of banking would create a financial strain.

But I wanted that job. New York is the nation's financial capital. The economy of the state is so enormous that if New York were a separate nation, it would rank as the ninth largest in the world. In other large states like California, savings and loans, credit unions and other kinds of banks are regulated by different departments; in New York, all financial institutions except for federally chartered commercial and savings banks fell under the jurisdiction of the superintendent. I would be controlling five hundred banks with $400 billion in assets and another $100 billion in trust accounts. I couldn't turn it down.

When the rumor about my appointment got out, a newspaper reporter asked if I thought a woman was capable of being the superintendent of banking. "Yes," I said, "the initials are S.O.B." But I had to cooperate with the state police on a background check. This included granting permission for an investigator to rifle through any records about my firm held by the Stock Exchange. And I had to appear for a two-hour confirmation hearing before the finance committee of the state senate, where I was expecting to confront a reporter who had recently gone after me: Years before, an analyst for my firm, Morton Sloane, had gotten the monthly production figures on an electronic-components company called CTS Corporation. Sloane had given these numbers to Dan Dorfman, who wrote a column called "Abreast of the Market" in *The Wall Street Journal,* on the condition that he not print them; the following day the exact figures were in the paper. CTS was embarrassed and angry and would now cut off any in-

formation to Siebert & Co.—maybe even sue. I had an angry conversation with Dorfman and vowed never again to trust him with
any proprietary information. When he heard the rumor that I was
to be appointed superintendent of banking and called me, I ob-
fuscated.

Once my name was made public, Dorfman wrote in *New
York* magazine that I had declared myself unfit for the job, and
he made several calls to Albany, to state senators and assemblymen, seemingly intent on blocking my confirmation. I was
warned that my hearing might get uncomfortable and, indeed,
one of the senators asked me to explain my comment in the
article. What I *had* said to Dorfman was that I was not a lawyer
and had never held a regulatory position, but because of the
notoriety attendant to buying my Big Board seat, I'd been
offered a number of jobs for which I had no experience. I also
let it be known that he was still angry about our conversation
regarding the CTS matter. "You're going to have to excuse my
language," I apologized in advance, "but I called him a fucking
liar to his face." The room erupted in laughter, and within minutes I was confirmed, unanimously but for one vote. An
African-American state senator named Carl McCall had questioned my firm's commitment to hiring women and minorities.
In my response, I mentioned one employee, nervously referring
to her as a "black girl."

"Most people in the forefront of the women's movement
don't use that word," McCall commented.

"I'm still flattered when *I'm* called a girl," I responded. I guess
this sounds awfully flip, even for 1977, but in those nascent days
of what came to be called feminism, there was so much stri-
dency, so much rhetoric, so many disagreeable leaders. I didn't
identify with them; I felt there were different ways for women to
go about demanding and achieving the opportunities to do what
we were capable of doing. But that was then. Today I consider
myself a friend and admirer of McCall, the first minority candidate elected to state office in New York, who did a great job as

state comptroller. And I am proud to say that, on a percentage basis, my firm probably has more women and minorities than any other firm on Wall Street.

I made a handshake agreement to serve through the 1978 election, less than two years away, but I ending up staying five years as the banking system was pushed to the brink of disaster. The governor said he'd hold the position for me until my mother's condition stabilized, though I would have to sign my oath before the legislature adjourned for the summer. Other open cabinet positions had been filled and the swearing-in parties held much earlier in the year. I went over to the banking department offices at the World Trade Center in New York City with bottles of champagne and a Bible on July 7: 7/7/77. An auspicious date (not that I was superstitious) Four days later, my mother died, never knowing about my new job.

There was some poetic justice that I was now regulating Morgan Guaranty, the bank that had refused me a loan to buy the seat on the Stock Exchange. I had to ask myself if I'd be able to regulate fairly an institution that had done business with my firm in the past, perhaps even treated me badly. (The answer was yes.) But there were some odd new relationships. When my mother was in the hospital, I'd leave my office down in the financial district, drive to see her and get home in time to park my car in front of Billy's—my favorite neighborhood restaurant, on First Avenue—at precisely seven o'clock, when the alternate-side-of-the-street regulations changed. One night I was at the bar waiting for a table and struck up a conversation with a man who asked if I was a regular customer.

"I've been coming here since it was up on Fifty-sixth Street," I said.

"No," he said, "it was on Third Avenue."

I called over the waitress, a woman I'd known for years. "Hermine," I asked, "where was the old place?"

"Four blocks up on Fifty-sixth Street," she said, "and I still have the clippings from the day you bought the seat."

The stranger's ears perked up. "You're the first woman member?" he asked. "You probably do a lot of business with us. I'm with Citibank."

"No," I said. "An honest broker can't get through your trading desk." Just then, a table became available, and I sat down for dinner. The gentleman waited until a table opened next to me. I was eating my rare roast beef with a baked potato when I heard him ask, "What did you mean?"

I explained that I had repeatedly gotten burned at Citibank ever since I started to discount commissions: If I received an order to sell 80,000 shares of a stock at $70, I'd offer it to clients, but another broker would mysteriously come in and take the block. I believed that it must be one of the new institutional accounts, not one of my old clients going behind my back. So I tried something: If I had 80,000 shares to sell, I would offer one new institution 79,800, another one 79,500, and another one 79,000. That way, when a buyer or seller came to the floor mentioning that figure, I would know where it had come from. Citibank picked me off three times. It was obvious that somebody there preferred to direct the business elsewhere.

Six weeks later, I was appointed superintendent of banking, and the man I'd been chatting with that night—William Spencer, the president of Citibank—called to congratulate his new boss.

It was daunting being called "the most powerful woman in New York" from as far away as the *Financial Times* of London, but I worried that, despite a successful career in securities, I had little direct banking experience. For the first few months I was in office, I set the alarm for 4:00 A.M. to plow through background information; in the evening. I did homework from dinner to bedtime. As it turned out, my tenure was marked by a host of new problems, and previous banking experience would have done me little good. For starters, the Municipal Credit Union for employees of the city of New York was in shambles, the target of barbs, innuendo, lawsuits and investigations. There was a bitter internecine battle on the board (I was told that some members had literally put guns on the table), and there had not been an annual meeting for four or five years. In August 1977 two MCU employees were arrested and charged with taking kickbacks on loan applications, one from a policeman.

In October a front-page article in the New York *Daily News* reported that MCU had $130 million in assets and the insurance fund of the National Credit Union Administration was only $95 million. I knew there would be problems, because if MCU went under, the insurance fund didn't have enough to pay the investors. The day the article appeared, there was the equivalent of a run on the bank: Hundreds of members made anxious calls about MCU's internal affairs, and withdrawals increased from a norm of just over $250,000 a day to $1.5 million. People were standing in line to take their money out, like a scene from *It's a Wonderful Life*. I had bank examiners going down to the credit union on lower Broadway to reassure people that their money was insured, and the next day I went too, shaking hands and introducing myself, careful to greet one black person, then one white person. People would say, "You look honest, lady, but this is my money." We were afraid they would get hit over the head leaving the building because muggers would know they had cash in their wallets, so I got Manufacturers Hanover Trust Co. to open up a temporary branch in the lobby. This way, they could take their money out of the credit union and put it right in a new Manny Hanny account, leaving the building with a nice safe deposit slip.

In November I notified Governor Carey that I had no choice but to take possession and rehabilitate the credit union. No superintendent of banking had done that since the Depression, but it was within our purview to do so. We could also have sold it, if there had been a buyer willing to take it, or declared it to be insolvent and turned it over to the Federal Insurance Agency. But that would have meant that the credit union that served the city and state employees working there would be no more. Instead, we fired all the officers, directors and top-echelon personnel and set about cleaning house. We instituted new, more stringent eligibility requirements for membership too. Forty percent of the shareholders had less than fifty dollars on account, but most loans had gone to those with minimum deposits, who often defaulted. In order to get the credit union's books and methods in good working order again, more than $5 million in loans given out by the former administration had to be swallowed.

By the beginning of 1979, we were ready to return control to the membership, but I certainly did not want the same people who had brought me Pearl Harbor—there was no indication that they would behave any differently the second time around. I signed an order prohibiting any of the two dozen incumbents from being reelected and named a five-man nominating committee to come up with a full slate of new candidates for the board. Some of the old directors were running around getting petitions signed, accusing me of being undemocratic, since no charges of wrongdoing had been filed. But in hindsight, my biggest mistake was excluding any city employees from the nominating committee. This engendered accusations of elitism, when all I was trying to do was get extremely qualified people to serve as "headhunters" for an efficient new board.

What I never expected was to be charged with racial discrimination. More than half the credit union's 100,000 members were black, as was Thomas Clark, a deputy banking superintendent whom I appointed executive director of the credit union when we took over. But four black incumbents barred from running for office brought suit, charging me with "diluting potential black strength" at the MCU and "trial by innuendo." These four men—Julian Garfield, Horace Mason, Warren Bright and David Rock—claimed that they had consistently presented the credit union's problems to the banking department (no one at the department ever agreed) and were now being condemned as whistle-blowers or found guilty by association with the inept board. My motive in all this, incidentally, was supposed to have been a personal vendetta against Carl McCall for having cast the lone vote against me in my confirmation hearings and for charging that I was insensitive to women and minorities. A state court issued an injunction overturning my decision and barring the election of a new board. The judge called my actions arbitrary, capricious and "constitutionally abhorrent."

I had thought I could avoid bringing charges against the suspended officers, and I didn't think it would accomplish anything to wash dirty linen in public, but the democratic process now demanded that I roll up my sleeves and take out my Wisk. I could have let them onto the ballot, but I refused to do that—I thought the shareholders were entitled to management that could be trusted, and I didn't know who on the old board had done what. Garfield, Mason and the others might have been the good guys, but the two competing factions had charged each other with various kinds of incompetence and kickbacks. Sometimes cleaning house is really dirty work.

I believe in rewarding excellence. When it came to promotions, I often passed over the first man in line, and if I didn't advance people in the right order, the examiners got mad. Once I sent a deputy back to the field—something that just wasn't done—but the man wasn't doing his job, so I bit the bullet. (That man later took early retirement—and got a job with a bank.) If problems or emergencies demanded more personnel or a specific talent in a certain area, I'd move people around, from

I believe in rewarding excellence.

Albany to Manhattan or vice versa. The deputies resented reassignment and threatened to sue, and I'd have to pay them a per diem. The bulk of the department's function was the examination process, but there were so many new banks to be examined that I needed a way to make the same number of people cover more territory. We used to examine banks every year, as did the federal authorities, so we did away with that redundancy. Now we alternated with the feds every other year. There often seemed to be a disconnect between my responsibilities and my resources. But the incident that created the most trouble and engendered the wrath of my boss involved an Asian bank that most people in New York State knew nothing about.

Much of my effort as superintendent was spent in arranging marriages between ailing and healthy banks. In 1978, when the Hong Kong and Shanghai Banking Company (HSBC) wanted to buy the Buffalo-based Marine Midland Bank, I first thought it was a great idea, but then resisted. It was becoming increasingly fashionable for major international banks to have a retail presence in this country. The decline of the dollar and the depressed price of undervalued American bank stocks made domestic banks an attractive investment for wealthy foreign investors, who also liked the political stability of this country and our managerial know-how. As a senior officer of the British Barclays Bank said, "We view the United States as the last bastion of capitalism. We feel our money's safe here." Overseas banks controlled more than 10 percent of U.S. banking assets. The French owned Bank of California, the Spanish owned Bank of Virginia, the Dutch owned LaSalle National of Chicago, the Brazilians owned Republic National of New York—each with over $1 billion in assets. But Marine, among the fifteen largest banks in the country, would be the plum. While it had an insignificant portion of assets in New York City, it was either the largest or second largest bank in every upstate area except Albany. Marine had gotten into trouble in the turbulence following the last recession and had emerged weakened and in need of capital, although it was not on our troubled list at that time. The obvious solution would have been a merger with another bank, but antitrust laws prohibited the merger of banks competing in the same markets, while other federal statutes prevented banks from crossing state lines. Since Marine was such a big operation, it was practically impossible for it to find a partner within the state that met the antitrust test. But more important, the bank was clearly on the mend.

HSBC was a $12 billion financial empire, so pervasive in the British Crown Colony of Hong Kong that it was known simply as "the Bank." It was so tightly wedded to the political establishment that it issued 85 percent of Hong Kong's currency, one of the few private scrips left in the world. HSBC had been the major financier of Imperial China, and even after the Communist takeover in 1949, it was fueled by the many Chinese entrepreneurs and workers who emigrated to Hong Kong from the People's Republic. (The Chinese name for the bank, Wayfoong, was a sign of appreciation; literally translated, it meant "abundance of remittances.") The bank's chairman was an unofficial member of the exclusive Executive Council, Hong Kong's equivalent of a cabinet post. (While the governor of the colony was the titular head of state, no one seriously questioned that the head of HSBC had more clout.) Upon becoming chairman in September 1977, Michael G. R. Sandberg and his wife, Carmel, moved into a new bank-financed mansion atop Victoria Peak, overlooking the Hong Kong harbor. The residence, with its twelve-car garage, was officially called Sky High (ostensibly referring to its location, not its price), but it was invariably known as "Carmelot" or "Costalot." HSBC was also spending an estimated $650 million to $1 billion on its new headquarters in Hong Kong. At the time, it was the most money spent on a single building anywhere.

Sandberg was a former British army officer whose "aw-shucks" self-deprecation hid his entrepreneurial drive. (Showing off his collection of antique pocket watches, including some erotic "action" models, Sandberg was fond of saying, "I buy these because I'm not smart enough to know if that vase over there is really a Ming.") He and his deputy chairman, John Boyer, another old colonial army hand, were said to operate in classic good cop/bad cop mode. "Sandberg tries to get the information out of you with cigarettes," said one business associate,

"while Boyer prefers sticking bamboo splinters under your fin-
gernails."

Sandberg was known more as a trader than a banker, a man
whose eyes lit up when he was brought a deal, and the one deal
said to obsess him was the bank's longtime plan for a major
presence in the United States. Shortly after assuming office, he
commissioned a study that moved Marine Midland to the top of
his target list. Sandberg met Marine chairman Edwin W. Duffy
for dinner at the Banker's Club in New York and found him
agreeable to a takeover. After another big powwow at the Kahala
Hilton in Hawaii (chosen for security reasons), HSBC announced its intentions of acquiring 51 percent of Marine for
about $260 million. Sandberg referred to Marine as "a jolly-
well-run bank," and all parties insisted on calling the arrangement a partnership. The deal would make HSBC a global giant,
catapulting it in size from seventy-seventh to thirty-fifth among
all world banks.

I didn't really care about Hong-Shang's executive perks or
real-estate indulgences. And I didn't subscribe to the theory of
an economic conspiracy against the United States by foreign
investors. "Marine Midland seeks the partnership to better
enable it to increase its business, especially in New York State,"
said Duffy, "and xenophobic attacks on investments from
abroad are pure jingoism and contrary to United States policy
and interests." (A *New York Post* reporter asked me, "How do
you feel about being called xenophobic?" I responded, "Wait
until I look it up in the dictionary.") As Carter Golembe, a
Washington, D.C., banking consultant put it, taking over the
U.S. financial system by buying a rather enfeebled bank holding
company with roots deepest in Buffalo could be likened to cap-
turing Chicago by landing eight hundred guerillas in Duluth,
Minnesota.

I was accused of many kinds of stupidity and cupidity. Some
speculated that I was ambitious for higher office and was making a fuss to raise my public profile, or that I was trying to

embarrass the governor because I was a Republican. (Politicking from my office had been the norm in previous administrations: a deputy told me that he used to keep track, for the superintendent, of how much banks were contributing to various campaigns.) Others thought I might be seeking revenge for some ancient slights against my brokerage by Salomon Bros., the investment bankers involved in the acquisition. (At a cocktail party, I shouted a friendly "Hi" to one of Salomon's M&A guys I'd known for years on the Street. "I shouldn't be talking to you," he growled. "You're costing us too much money.") It was reported that I considered HSBC's managers anti-Semitic because its most profitable subsidiary, the British Bank of the Middle East, had strong ties to Arab oil money and had observed the recent Arab boycott.

And I was said to be miffed because when HSBC embarked on the merger, officials from the Fed were formally invited to Hong Kong but not me. (The offer had been casual—on the order of "Why don't you come over and see us?"—and Sandberg said he was surprised that nobody from New York State came to look over his operations.) It was also suggested that, however tenacious my efforts to block the deal, my *real* intent was to use the HSBC application as a platform from which to win support for changes in U.S. banking laws and regulations that gave foreign banks an edge over domestic banks in takeover situations; that I wanted the financial community to reflect on the question of increasing foreign ownership and to change the rules.

These charges were a politician's way of thinking. Quite simply, I was worried that the HSBC would not meet the needs of the local communities where Marine Midland was a unique institution, with the largest branch system upstate. When a bank was as dominant in an area as Marine was in northern New York, a change in lending policies could have several adverse effects on the local economy. If international loans appeared more profitable than loans in Buffalo or nearby Rochester, chances were the local deposits would be used for lending in far-flung places. There would be nothing to stop the foreign bank from "upstreaming" Marine's capital to one of the companies it owned, thus draining resources from the communities where the banks operated. I was concerned about the fungibility of bank assets: If, let's say, foreigners bought U.S. Steel, the company's assets would still remain solidly here. But a foreign buyer of a U.S. bank could use domestic deposits to make loans without any consideration of local requirements.

The highly unusual terms of the proposed transaction raised other concerns: There was an offer to stockholders related to market value and an infusion of funds into the bank at closest to book value, meaning that Marine's shareholders were receiving about 50 percent less for their shares than HSBC was paying for new shares to be purchased from the bank. I still didn't think the stockholders got a fair deal in the two-pronged pricing. I had been on Wall Street for more than twenty years, and not once had I seen a deal where new money had gone into a company at a 50 percent higher price than what stockholders had gotten for some of their shares at the same time. It's true that nothing was forced down their throats. They voted loudly in favor—in fact, the offering was oversubscribed. But that was not an adequate indication of fair dealing. Any time that people are paid more than the market price, they're going to jump in.

I had decided against the monumental task of requiring HSBC to supply financial data based upon U.S. accounting rules, and the information I did receive about its plans and operations was far less than I would normally get from a bank in my jurisdiction. Yet when I requested more, I was refused. HSBC wouldn't give us a list of stockholders—said it was none of our business—and acted exasperated at our requests. "Our soul has been bared to them," said Sandberg. "I mean, you can't go to a bank regulatory and say, 'Piss off.'" The government of the Crown Colony was fully behind Hong-Shang's policy of utter secrecy about its "inner reserves": a portion of each year's earnings that were not reported to shareholders as a cushion against yo-yoing share prices or calamities such as war that could undermine depositor confidence. Sandberg's distinctly British terminology for any ominous concerns about such practices was *codswallop*. "After Watergate," he asserted in one interview, "anything that is not disclosed in America has an aura not just of mystery but of something not smelling quite right."

The Asian bank's tentacles reached around the globe into all sorts of nonbanking businesses—carpets, hotels, farming, films, newspapers, breweries, quarrying, shipping, insurance, timber, Cathay Pacific Airways—in all, almost four hundred subsidiaries in more than sixty different businesses in forty countries. The nonfinancial business interests of HSBC were so extensive that there was some question as to whether it was principally engaged in banking. It was not inconceivable that Hong-Shang could cause money to be diverted to companies where it had a piece of the action. In this country, federal prohibitions made it impossible for U.S. businesses to have such diversification and gave a wildly unfair advantage to foreign competitors. Virtually alone among major industrial nations, the United States required a strict separation of banking and nonbanking activities, reflecting a fear that if banks got into other businesses, they might take unnecessary risks with depositors' money.

Marine was one of the fifteen largest U.S. banks, and when HSBC first appeared on the scene, it was still listed by the U.S. Comptroller of the Currency as a "problem bank." But the crisis was long past, the smaller bank having lifted itself up by its own bootstraps. By the time the merger was consummated, profits from banking operations were up 41 percent over the previous year's; both earnings and capital were on sharp upward curves. Management had corrected problems, and had caught up on delinquent loans. Chairman Duffy received a 32.7 percent salary increase from Marine Midland the same year that the merger with Hong-Shang was broached.

The many members of the Independent Bankers Association of New York State were also up in arms over the merger. Henry G.

Waltemade, chairman of the board of the Dollar Savings Bank of
New York, pointed out how takeovers by foreign banks could affect employment, since there was no guarantee that the new owners would not gradually substitute their own employees. Howard
Coughlin, president of the Office and Professional Employees International Union, raised the issue that when European American
Bank took over Franklin Bank, the latter's staffers were treated as
new workers for purposes of all fringe benefits, including pen-
sions. I got a call of support from Peter Cook at the Bank of England, which had denied HSBC permission to buy the Royal Bank
of Scotland. And the Canadian government rejected HSBC's proposal to acquire two Marine branches in Toronto, citing its failure
to "meet the test of significant benefit to Canada," as defined by
the country's Foreign Investment Review.

Joining me in my opposition was an ally I didn't need: a radical political group called the U.S. Labor Party, whose goals and
finances were shrouded in mystery. The group's leader, Lyndon
H. LaRouche, Jr., had called himself "Lyn Marcus" (a combina-
tion of *Lenin* and *Marx*) in the '60s and was seldom referred to
in the press without the use of the word *fringe* or *wacko*. He
claimed that the Holocaust was a "common delusion of the
American Zionist," that Henry Kissinger was a Soviet agent and
(most germane to my situation) that HSBC financed an international drug trade. Hong-Shang was supposed to be the original
dope-laundering bank set up following the end of the second
British Opium War in 1860. Several times LaRouche called my
office to warn that I'd be murdered if I went to Britain, where I
was planning a trip to discuss foreign bank regulation with the
British authorities. HSBC officials, in return, declared that the
KGB was behind this attempt to scuttle the merger, insisting that
the Soviets had more to gain than anyone else from embarrassing Hong Kong and attributing the timing of the attack to the
opening of the debate in Washington about establishing relations with China. LaRouche went on to be convicted of fraud
and tax conspiracy during the Reagan Administration, a felony

that he wore like a badge of honor, contending that the charges were part of a government attempt to "eliminate" him.

I wrote to Representative Henry S. Reuss, the Democratic head of the House Banking Committee, urging a congressional investigation of foreign bank takeovers. Already forty-seven U.S. banks with $19 billion in domestic assets were under foreign ownership, and they were not subject to the same restrictions and reporting requirements that applied to American institutions. There were constant rumors of other foreign bank acquisitions waiting in the wings (two of them British), and if the trend continued, I was wary about much too much foreign control of our banking industry.

"I am well aware that the home countries of the acquiring banks in the matters before us would have fits if Americans would try to take over their banking institutions," admitted Reuss in an interview. It was taken for granted that the Bank of England, for instance, would not permit foreigners to acquire a majority position of a British clearing bank or accepting house (roughly the equivalent of our investment banks). Actually, my department had contacted every major central bank in the world and found it highly unlikely that the banking authorities of *any* other major country would permit one of their largest banks, comparable to Marine Midland in size or relative share of its markets, to be sold off to deep-pocketed foreigners.

G. William Miller, chairman of the Fed, disagreed and approved the HSBC merger in March 1979. But I still had veto power, and I wasn't giving in—the Fed had its criteria, and I had mine. In May, State Commerce Secretary John Dyson publicly intimated that I would be fired if I rejected the plan over what he considered the clear interests of the state. (*The New York Times* quoted him as saying that the governor had dismissed past officials for "the virulent disease of regulationitis.") Dyson was generally considered to be a public sounding board for Carey's private views and was responsible for several departures from the current administration. It would do no good to get into a mud-slinging contest with him, but I was determined to hang tough. When he stated that Marine needed infusions of new capital, I wrote him a letter noting that anybody who spread rumors undermining the state's banking system was committing a misdemeanor under state law.

I'd been dealing with Bob Morgado, the governor's aide, from the beginning of my tenure. When I arrived at the banking department, I'd tried calling Carey a few times and discovered that it was Morgado who would call back. State commissioners and assemblymen hated him because he did Carey's dirty work—he was invariably known as the Shadow Governor, the Ayatollah of Albany or, since he was Hawaiian-born, the Pineapple. Now he started issuing vaguely ominous statements about a possible "restructuring" of the banking department. He spoke to the *Times* about doing some staff "housecleaning" to get more "speed" and "flexibility" in the administration, promising that several (unnamed) people would be "launched into space pretty soon." The *Daily News* mentioned as my replacement Bess Myerson, former Miss America, former commissioner of consumer affairs for New York City and frequent hostess for bachelor Mayor Ed Koch.

One banking executive called to say he'd heard on the radio that I was unhappy in my job and would be returning to my firm. I told him that wasn't true. Then I got a tape of the radio program and played it at an executive session of the banking board, which promptly passed a resolution in my honor and sent it to the governor's office. When Warren Anderson, the majority leader of the state senate, heard about this from a bank officer, he sent senate counsel John Hagarty to see Morgado. "If you fire her," Hagarty warned, "you're not going to get anyone else confirmed." The governor's own brother lived in my building. One day he whispered to me in the lobby, "I understand you're having problems. Call me before you quit."

On May 10, I was scheduled to have a three o'clock meeting with Morgado at the governor's midtown office. At two-thirty, just as I was getting ready to go uptown, I got a call from Bob Bennett, a *New York Times* reporter who covered the banking industry, saying that I was going to be fired at three o'clock.

Morgado always put his feet up on his desk, so that anyone talking to him was looking at the soles of his shoes. That day I purposely wore a red pantsuit with short black alligator boots so I could put my feet up on his desk too.

"Stop screwing around and approve the deal, period," he said.

"Are you ordering me?" I asked.

"Yes."

One thought was going through my head: *Stay tough.* "Bob," I said, "you've got my job."

When I left his office, there was a reporter from *American Banker* sitting in the hall. "Are you still employed?" he asked.

I turned around, went back to Morgado's office and said, "I think you'd better talk to this guy."

What Morgado knew at the time, but I did not, was that banking and insurance are the only departments of New York State government run by superintendents, not commissioners, who are appointed by the governor but do not serve at his pleasure. Morgado could make it miserable for me but couldn't fire me. For the first time ever, auditors were dispatched to the banking department, ostensibly because of my requests for a budget

Stay tough.

to cover our many new consumer-related activities. And I certainly wasn't invited when the governor married Evangeline "Engie" Gouletas in April 1981. (Her family controlled American Invesco, the nation's largest converter of apartments into condominiums. She was discovered to have had an extra ex-husband, previously unmentioned, prompting bumper stickers that said, "Honk if you've ever been married to Engie.")

The only tangible result of my efforts was that HSBC had to pay shareholders another five dollars when the deal went through, beyond my control. Marine Midland applied for a national charter, thereby doing an end run around my jurisdiction. (It had become legal for state institutions to apply for federal charters in 1978.) Salomon handled the deal—self-reverentially referring to itself as a "gladiator" on behalf of the principals—and in February 1980 the initials *N.A.* for National Association were added to the bank's official name. (To get a bank charter in New York, a foreign interest must pledge some kind of reciprocal arrangement for a New York bank in the applicant's country. The U.S. Comptroller of the Currency imposes no such requirement for granting a federal charter, and where none is required, none is offered.) John G. Heimann, the decidedly pro-international C of the C who had preceded me as superintendent of banking, conceded that exempting foreigners from rules about nonbanking activities inevitably meant inconsistency. But he claimed that it was a "practical" response to wide variations between domestic and overseas practices. Insisting that a foreign bank holding company divest itself of its extracurricular activities, he said, would be viewed as discrimination and invite retaliation against our banks abroad. Heimann quoted Alexander Hamilton to the effect that "rather than treating the foreign investor as a rival, we should consider him a valuable helper," and went on to say that "those who, by restricting foreign investment would tamper with the underlying precepts of our system, must bear the burden of proof."

The proof for me was that, in the years after regulatory approval came through, Marine Midland indeed became less interested in upstate New York, aiming at a different image: that of a chic international financial institution. Foreign was in. Nobody was taking pride in making more mortgages in Buffalo. One large real estate developer in the area who had dealt with the Marine system for nearly forty years was bitterly disappointed when he called me. The new bank management was under great bottom-line pressure, he said, which had ultimately brought to a standstill the redevelopment of the downtown

Binghamton area, in which his firm played a major role. He cited a general movement of funds out of the region, which was now literally being starved for credit. This left the community to deal with storefront banks that had no sense of civic responsibility. An officer of Corning Glass told me that he'd had to call Marine Midland's chairman Duffy personally to get a loan for one of the company's suppliers.

The Hong-Shang people were publicly polite about my dissent, probably realizing they had to live with me. "As a woman," Michael Sandberg said in an interview, "she must have had a much tougher path to the top on Wall Street than if she'd been a man." In October 1980, he even invited me to a party at the elegant Pierre Hotel celebrating the centenary of HSBC's New York office. (I didn't go.) An editor at the *Journal of Commerce*, which had criticized me for my decision about Marine, called me in August 1983 and said that in the next day's edition, there would be an editorial with the headline: WAS MURIEL SIEBERT RIGHT? Two years after the merger, Morgado came under fire for accepting $280,000 in low-interest loans to build a baronial house near Albany. It was revealed that $100,000 of that sum had been a loan from a millionaire real-estate developer who was a heavy Carey campaign contributor *and* held more than $10 million in state contracts. The remaining $180,000 was from Marine Midland. New York Attorney General Robert Abrams questioned whether Morgado should have taken the mortgage at all, let alone at an interest rate several points below the prevailing 18 percent at the time of his closing, considering his earlier involvement in championing the bank.

Morgado ended up as head of Warner Music Group, then was fired as part of the corporate bloodbath there after the Time-Warner merger. He was reportedly paid $60 million to leave the company. HSBC is on virtually every block of New York City now. Needless to say, my own accounts are elsewhere.

• • •

Political concern about the incursion of foreign interests into the American banking system was hardly new. Andrew Jackson had played on similar nationalistic emotion 150 years before when he had vetoed a charter for the Second Bank of the United States. "Should the stock of the bank principally pass into the hands of the subjects of a foreign country, and we should unfortunately become involved in a war with that country, what would be our condition?" he asked. "All its operations within would be in aid of the hostile fleets and armies without." In 1923 the New York State Senate threw out a bill that would have allowed foreign banks to establish branches in the city, and no change was made until 1961.

My concerns were less hysterical, but it was hard to ignore the patchwork of regulations that offered unfair advantages to foreign banks: Banking rules dating back to Alexander Hamilton and the First Bank of the United States favored local state-by-state control. Germans could buy a bank in Wisconsin that a Louisiana bank would be prohibited from buying. And it would be a near-impossible task to have federal examiners beyond U.S. frontiers to supervise foreign institutions and analyze their books so as to ensure their soundness, unless the home government of that bank complied. But even when records were made available, it could be much more difficult to spot and review intercorporate transactions that might be adverse to the safety of the bank.

Certain rules of reciprocity were established under the International Banking Act of 1978, which mandated that a foreign bank ought to be able to do the same kind of business in this country that U.S. banks could do in the home of the foreigner. (Hong Kong, for example, had a twelve-year moratorium on new foreign bank branches, which was lifted just eight days before the announcement of the proposed Marine Midland acquisition. A year later, the moratorium was reimposed.) But this law did not really address the issue of acquisition of large American banks by foreigners. There was not a single instance of any major country in the world allowing control of a large domestic bank to pass into the hands of a U.S. bank. Another factor that warranted consideration was that many foreign banks were government owned or controlled, operating in closer harmony with their political leadership than was (or is) the case in this country. I was concerned about the results of a questionnaire I had sent to twenty central banks throughout the world, which revealed that very few had deposit insurance. In several cases, voluntary pools of funds had been set up for this purpose to protect customers. I argued strenuously for Federal Deposit Insurance Corporation (FDIC) coverage of deposits in U.S. branches of foreign banks, even though many of them were unhappy about the cost and the perception that American depositors would be treated better than their own nationals. People putting their money in a bank on American soil were entitled to the same protection, no matter how far away the home office. Equal powers imply commensurate responsibilities. Since insurance protection was most important for the life savings of individual citizens, I accepted the compromise fashioned in the U.S. Senate, requiring FDIC coverage only for deposits of under $100,000. A sort of emotional tertiary concern, much less amenable to regulation, was the distinct possibility that foreign bank parents would pay less attention to the development, growth and economic well-being of the areas where they operated in this country than an institution owned by American citizens.

In July 1979 I testified about all of this in front of the U.S. Senate's Banking Committee and, about two weeks later, the House Subcommittee on Commerce, Consumer and Monetary Affairs, urging the development of a national policy toward foreign acquisitions. I urged support of the Foreign Bank Takeover Act introduced by Senator William Proxmire, a Wisconsin Democrat, and Senator John Heinz, a Pennsylvania Republican. The bill would impose a moratorium on foreign acquisitions of U.S. banks with assets of at least $100 million, pending a study analyzing the impact of such takeovers on competition, credit and monetary policy. Congress did enact a temporary three-month moratorium in April 1980 (the Marine Midland deal slipped in just before), but when it was allowed to expire, the shopping spree resumed in earnest. Only days after the stopgap ban was no longer in effect, the British announced an agreement to gain majority control of Crocker National Bank of San Francisco, the fourteenth largest bank in the United States, with assets topping $16 billion. Five years later, the Treasury Department would announce that Crocker had been fined $2.25 million for failing to report cash transactions totaling almost $4 billion, transactions that the government believed were linked to the illegal narcotics trade. Under particular scrutiny was the nature of more than $3 billion in unreported funds originating in Hong Kong. The violations were said to be systematic and pervasive, involving twenty-nine branches, including two on the Mexican border. "What we are seeing is a higher degree of probability with Crocker that dirty money or narcotics money is being laundered through the institutions," said John M. Walker, Jr., the assistant treasury secretary for enforcement and operations. The Treasury was finally admitting to the Hong Kong dope connection that had been broached at the time of the HSBC deal. "We have a huge volume of Southeast Asian heroin that is coming into this country," said Walker, "and we know that a large number of deals are financed out of Hong Kong." He noted that law enforcement officials had a rough time getting information from Hong Kong banks about the source of money coming into the United States. The Hong Kong transactions appeared to be evidence of large-scale money laundering by international heroin traffickers, said Treasury officials. The lawyer for Crocker called these remarks "inflammatory" and "bordering on irresponsibility," insisting that the violations had been honest mistakes resulting from changes in the Bank Secrecy Act of 1970.

By the summer of 1980, the General Accounting Office, the watchdog arm of Congress, issued a recommendation for a further temporary ban on foreign acquisition of U.S. banks. At issue, it said, was national determination of a point at which foreign control of U.S. banking assets becomes worrisome and the U.S. laws that allow foreigners to purchase some U.S. banks that other U.S. banks aren't permitted to buy. The imbalance had to be righted.

If Americans were increasingly sensitive about foreign influence over the economy, the subject was doubly touchy when the foreigners were Arabs, as I learned when I later came to tangle with the Middle Eastern investors trying to establish a foothold in U.S. banking and with the eminent American who was trying to facilitate their effort. Clark M. Clifford was a superlawyer (the first in Washington to make a million dollars a year), a consummate political insider and *eminence grise* who had carried out many high-profile and behind-the-scenes assignments for Democratic presidents. A close confidant of Harry Truman—and organizer of the president's weekly poker game—Clifford recognized that Truman needed the political support of the American Jewish community in the 1948 election, and he counseled recognizing the new Jewish state of Israel the moment it declared independence. This went against the express wishes of Secretary of State (and war hero) George Marshall and the U.S. delegation to the United Nations, who threatened to resign en masse. Clifford went on to help formulate the policies for the reconstruction of Europe after World War II—the Truman Doctrine, the Marshall Plan and the North Atlantic Treaty Organization— and in 1968 he succeeded Robert McNamara as secretary of defense for the final ten months of the Lyndon Johnson administration. He spent that time warning against the folly of the Vietnam War.

From his law offices across the street from the White House, Clifford liked to think of himself as a bridge between business and government, often helping clients to navigate their way through legal obstacle courses. President Jimmy Carter turned to Clifford in 1977 when Carter's budget director, a Georgia buddy named Bert Lance, got in trouble over his banking practices back home. It was Lance who introduced Clifford to a group of Middle Eastern investors called Credit and Commerce American Holdings who were attempting a hostile takeover of Financial General Bankshares, a multistate holding company with $2.7 billion in twelve U.S. banks. With Lance's help, the Arab cartel (controlled, in part, by Sheikh Kamal Adham, former director of Saudi intelligence) bought 19.6 percent of FGB's stock. That 19.6 was significant: SEC regulations stipulated that any individual or group must make a public disclosure whenever 5 percent or more of a company's outstanding shares was bought. In what certainly appeared to be an attempt to bypass the law on a technicality, four members of the Arab consortium each bought 4.9 percent of FGB's stock.

Financial General filed a lawsuit to thwart the takeover, and the SEC filed charges, ordering that the cartel either make a public offer for the holding company or sell its shares. But in July 1980 Clifford was able to negotiate a settlement known as a "consent decree," in which the cartel agreed to offer 158.3 percent of the book value of FGB's shares to existing stockholders. The tender offer could not be made until all the necessary regulatory approvals were obtained. By September 1981, that process had been completed in Tennessee, Virginia and Maryland, but two of FGB's banks were in New York—the Bank of Commerce and Community State Bank—which is why Clifford and his younger partner, Robert A. Altman, appeared before me at a banking department hearing.

Clifford was silver-haired and silver-tongued, disciplined (he supposedly smoked *one* cigarette a day) and elegant (his French cuffs were half an inch longer than the sleeves of his impeccably tailored double-breasted suit). He understood perfectly the public furor over the proposed takeover but swore that it resulted from a "lack of understanding" on the part of the public. "This is a passive investment by these investors," he said. "They do not intend to run the property. . . . It will be an entirely American operation. In each instance we have asked the management to stay on, and they have agreed to do so. . . . We know that the value of the individual banks is the place that they occupy in their community. It is our belief that the takeover will result in stronger banks, in better service to the communities and that we will continue to adhere to the highest kind of ethical conduct with reference to this banking operation."

State Senator Manfred Ohrenstein took the stand with passionate opposition to the proposed takeover. While the United States provided easy entry to its financial systems, he argued, the same could hardly be said for the restrictive policies of Kuwait, the United Arab Emirates and Saudi Arabia, where the proposed investors were citizens. They were all closely tied to the governments of these countries—just how closely couldn't be determined since the principals had not fully disclosed the names of all participants backing the scheme, invoking confidentiality— and it was a mistake to allow agents of foreign governments to participate in the state's banking industry without total disclosure. It was, he maintained, the charter of FGB that made it a uniquely valuable acquisition despite its relatively limited assets, since it was one of only six U.S. banks that could operate in more than one state. Such a charter would give the bank opportunities to take advantage of different state laws and push money around. It was worth a fortune. "There is no reason," Ohrenstein testified, "for us to grant the competitive edge of an interstate charter to a group of investors whose political and economic interests may be contrary to the interests of the people of New York State."

It's amazing how emotional dry financial matters can become when there are human faces and conditions attached. Will Maslow, general counsel of the American Jewish Congress, expressed concerns that Arab control of two New York banks might lead to religious, racial or sexual discrimination. (His point was not unfounded; some Arab banks with deposits in U.S. banks were issuing checks marked "Valid in all countries of the world except Israel." American banks honoring such checks would be participating in the Arab boycott of Israel.) In contrast was the testimony of Dr. M. T. Mehdi, president of the American Arab Relations Committee, arguing that there should be no political consideration with regard to approval of the takeover. All that should be considered was the economic and public interest of New York and the United States. People were holding up maps showing that the Middle East was ten thousand miles away—the point being that such distant ownership could hardly mean appropriate domestic leadership. There were people challenging whether or not Clark Clifford was in fact an agent of a foreign government, in which case the Justice Department would have to get involved.

No one was more adamant in her opposition than State Senator Carol Berman, who came with the signatures of thousands of her constituents in Nassau and Queens counties. "This is not a group of ordinary investors who have simply spotted a good property at a low price," she said. "If their motive were simply to make money, then they surely would not be continuing through a tedious four-year regulatory agency process. . . . Maybe we should look toward who these people are for a clue as to why they show such diligence in pursuing these banks." The investors were all wealthy men with ties to oil, and control of the American banks would further strengthen the OPEC (Organization of Petroleum Exporting Countries) oil cartel through lines of credit. "They could simply demand that customers for their oil be forced to finance their purchase through FGB," she postulated, "which would give them interest income and further control over who gets to buy the oil. . . . Through the Washington area banks, the Arabs will be able to learn the intimate details about private dealings of its depositors, many of whom are important government officials. . . . Of course," said Berman, "the investors, being clever people, have hired representatives in

America who are also clever, not withstanding their first mistake with Lance. Not only clever but distinguished. In fact, these are some of the most well-known names in politics, government and the military that have been active in this century." But, she pointed out somewhat indelicately, "the distinguished citizens who are being used as legal advisors and members of the FGB board of directors all have one other thing in common: They are all over seventy years of age, so they can hardly be in a position to give us long-term assurances."

What nobody at the hearings was saying specifically was that the Bank of Commerce was known as a "Jewish" bank: Its big depositors were in Manhattan's diamond district and garment center. Examiners from my department had talked with people who held the larger accounts, all of whom said that if control of the bank went to a group that included the former head of Saudi intelligence, they would pull their money out. One of the people who made that promise was the Bank of Commerce's largest depositor; such a withdrawal could have sent the bank into a nosedive. But the outrage on the part of the Jewish bank customers was matched by indignation in the Arab community. I was getting calls from the Palestinian delegation at the U.N. saying that I had no business even holding public hearings. At one point, Clark Clifford came into my office. "You're withholding approval because there are so many Jews in the banking department," he said dramatically. "I want you to know that I have the pen Truman used to sign the document recognizing the state of Israel." I explained that the Jewish people in the banking department were evenhanded professionals. We had chartered the Iranian and the Saudi banks, as well as other banks owned by Muslims.

The whole situation could have been made even more complicated by the fact that Governor Carey had borrowed $750,000 from the Bank of Commerce for a congressional race, money that was still not repaid. To his extreme credit, he stayed out of the matter entirely. But the laws pertaining to the takeover were pretty clear, and the Arabs were in compliance, so my recommendation to the state banking board was that the takeover be approved. The board consisted of six members from the financial community and six members of the public. Eight votes were needed to approve the CCAH bid, and in November 1981 the vote was a five-to-five split, with one abstention and one absentee. Most of the banking members voted for approval; the nay votes were cast by the public members of the board. (Yes, I know this sounds as if the bankers were operating out of self-interest, but the bankers knew the rules, while the public was acting emotionally.) Clifford reproached me, saying, "Madame Superintendent, I was in the audience for the hearing, and you did not try hard enough." It was true—my heart wasn't in it. The investors insisted that their interest in acquiring Financial General was in no way diminished by the action of the banking board and vowed to find a way around the veto. What eventually cleared the way was a caveat to the deal: The Arabs had to sell the Bank of Commerce. Directors of that bank formed a group to purchase Financial General's majority share in the Bank of Commerce. The banking board gave its approval in March 1982. FGB was renamed First American Bankshares, and Clifford became its chairman.

Ten years later, the district attorney's office of New York City disclosed evidence that CCAH, the parent company of First American, was secretly controlled by the Bank of Credit and Commerce International. BCCI's massive loans securing First American's stock had never been disclosed to the Fed. Clifford himself had made about $6 million profit from bank stock that he had bought with an unsecured loan from BCCI. A grand jury was convened to determine whether Clifford and Altman had deliberately misled federal regulators when the two men assured them that BCCI would have no control. Describing BCCI as a global criminal operation, prosecutors shut it down in July 1991. The U.S. press would call it the biggest bank fraud in history. In 1992 the Federal Reserve charged Clifford and Altman with fraud, conspiracy and bribe-taking. I was called to testify before the grand jury, really for educational purposes, explaining to people who had never been informed about such matters what a bank is, how it's regulated, what's the purpose of the system. Clifford spent the remainder of his days on his legal defense, but in 1993, after he suffered a heart attack following quadruple bypass surgery, criminal charges against him were dropped, with the judge citing his age and failing health. He settled the last of the civil claims against him from the BCCI scandal (giving up millions in legal fees and First American stock) only days before his death in 1998 at the age of ninety-one. Altman was subsequently acquitted after a four-month trial in New York.

Perched on a shelf behind my desk on the thirty-second floor of the World Trade Center was a brightly painted wooden figure of a lion with a tamer's body horizontally suspended in midair and his head in the lion's mouth—a gift from my staff on my second anniversary as S.O.B. I fought hard, both in Albany and at the Federal Reserve in Washington, for measures that would make possible the creation of an international banking zone (IBZ) in the United States. Domestic units would be created within our larger, more globally oriented banks that could conduct the business of gathering funds from and making loans to nonresidents, free of the Fed's reserve requirements and interest-rate restrictions. American banks and branches and agencies of foreign banks would return international transactions to our own shores, giving the United States a piece of the action in the lucrative world of "offshore" banking. It did not make good financial or regulatory sense to force our banks to conduct certain kinds of business in Caribbean "shell" operations, and the IBZ would be able to keep that business at home.

In fall 1981, the zone became reality. Within six months it had drawn more than $100 billion in funds from other countries, with the bulk coming to New York. Of the 140 IBFs that announced they were going into business, 100 were in New York City. Some financial "authorities" such as *Institutional Investor* declared the IBZ a failure. It's true that the expected number of jobs never materialized, but a lot of red tape and unnecessary regulation were eliminated.

Despite my vocal opposition to some of the foreign encroachers, I presided over a huge influx of foreign banks into this country, quietly granting charters for fifty of them to set up shop in New York, particularly to serve large ethnic communities. From a questionnaire sent to foreign banks, I tried to ascertain any barriers to foreign ownership and operation of commercial banking facilities in the United States. The banking department never even had a deputy in charge of foreign banks—they were tucked in under another category, the large commercial banks—and I used to hear that the officials felt unwelcome coming into the department. When a new bank opened, the examiners sent in were goodwill ambassadors, while ensuring that laws were obeyed. It was our goal to get them off to a good start by explaining the rules and practices. Other countries held bank regulators in higher esteem because it was a lifetime career, whereas our best people would leave government for more lucrative opportunities. I tried to get the examiners' jobs upgraded. I went in with charts and graphs showing that we were losing good people to the higher salaries of federal examiners. We had the blessings of the banks, which were willing to pay for the raises. But the budget office objected, on the grounds that upgrades would have to be done across all the state agencies. Civil Service overruled Budget, but then the governor's office said no way, so it was no. One of the Civil Service commissioners told me that Morgado had called and said, "You gave away the whole store."

The chairmen of the largest banks in the world would pay courtesy calls on my office out of respect. Almost every week I met with representatives of countries wishing to open branches in New York State. The Japanese in particular didn't know quite how to handle a woman in my position, but they always brought sacks of small electronics, like calculators and alarm clocks; the staff would grab them but save one or two for me. They also introduced me to the fine points of eating sushi, like showing me how the chef would bounce a piece of raw fish on the counter to determine its freshness.

When the representative of the Hungarian bank came in to get licensing for an office and learned that my mother had come from Hungary, he started speaking the language. I stopped him. I know two words: *mudjah*, which means "Hungarian" (Magyar), and *nem*, which means "No." He certainly didn't want to hear them used together. By the time he returned, he had found a detailed history of my mother's family, things that I had never known because the family didn't talk much about life in Europe. They had owned a leather tannery in the old country that burned down, taking much of the town with it. My grandfather often negotiated a way out of the army for smart young men who wanted to find their fortune in the new world, sometimes paying their way to America. Most of them settled in Cleveland, and when Ben, the eldest of the family's eight living children, immigrated to the United States in 1872, he chose Ohio to be near others from his hometown. Uncle Ben brought his siblings over as he could afford it; my mother, at age one, was in the third and final wave in 1892. Of the extended family who stayed in Europe, only two were alive after World War II. I remember when my mother got that phone call.

I believed that foreign banks should be allowed to expand in the United States only in the same way that American banks were allowed to expand in the foreign bank's home country. I begged the Bank of China to allow one of our banks to open a branch in Beijing or Shanghai so that I could declare reciprocity and allow the Chinese to establish a New York branch. Hoping to get a better feeling for the culture that might enhance my powers of persuasion, I went to China in the summer of 1979. A New York friend named Ernest Chu, whose aunt had been mayor of Shanghai, sent telexes to the people he thought I should meet. His missives were extravagant in their praise, claiming, "Madame Siebert has conquered a great world of total discrimination."

One of these messages was sent to Madame Sun Yat-sen, widow of the founding father of the Republic of China. The country had only recently been opened to tourism, and all trips were arranged by the national travel agency, Quo Fung, whose representatives met me in Hong Kong. I got off the plane wearing white jeans with a T-shirt and sneakers, and did exactly what I'd been instructed to do, which was to present my handwritten letter of introduction. The guide meeting me was flabbergasted that a person with such an abandonment of personal deportment was going to meet such an important woman as Madame Sun Yat-sen. Once I arrived on the mainland, I was driven to her home and shown to her bedroom, where the eighty-six-year-old woman was reclining next to a tank of oxygen. She spoke beautiful English and wanted to discuss the relative safety of New York subways.

It was virtually impossible to walk down the street without someone asking if he or she could speak to me in English. Everyone seemed delighted to shake hands, and the children wanted to touch my exotic (blond) hair. If I had an address written on a piece of paper, some man, woman or child would show me the way, invariably walking me to the location. The Bank of China had arranged for a banquet in my honor, but nobody told me that the Chinese dressed down for such occasions, hoping to make the guest of honor feel comfortable, so it was something of a gaffe that I was wearing evening clothes. I was asked if I wanted a fork, and my hosts seemed pleased that I declined, preferring to eat with chopsticks. The meal consisted of more than thirty separate courses, with a toast of strong drink and the words *Goom-bai* ("Down the hatch") between each course. I was given a box of dates to ensure a return to China, like throwing a coin in Rome's Trevi Fountain.

My goodwill trip notwithstanding, the Bank of China declared, "No reciprocity." No American bank would be permitted to open in China. Like Hong-Shang, the Chinese sought a federal charter to circumvent New York State laws. The disgraceful competition between federal and state regulators created a loophole that allowed an inherent inequity to exist. I sued the Comptroller of the Currency for usurping our powers, and the conference of state bank superintendents joined in the suit, but we lost—I think because of the inflexible state attorney general who wouldn't allow me to hire top-quality outside counsel. It was not realistic to expect someone from the attorney general's office to be an expert in the specific laws relevant to this case, and there was too short a period of time to learn what was needed. But this was not the sort of case the states should have lost.

There were four Iranian banks with branches in New York, and I had chartered all of them. In 1978 I was invited to Iran on the occasion of the fiftieth anniversary of Bank Melli, the most prominent of these, with offices in the General Motors building on Fifth Avene. The other Americans were all high-ranking bank officers, as the Iranians had accounts and relationships with the largest financial institutions in this country. But out of a list of almost one hundred official guests—from Morocco to Venezuela, from the USSR to Sri Lanka, from Bulgaria to Bahrain—I was the only woman. (A preliminary questionnaire was sent, requesting me to check if I would be traveling alone or "accompanied by wife.")

I knew that the trip could be considered dangerous—anti-American sentiment in Iran was already palpable—and I kept calling the State Department to see if it was safe, but I joked that if things got tough, I'd hire a plane and fly myself out. (People who know how to fly always think they have an out, although if a major airline was having trouble leaving the country, it might have been just a little difficult for me to get a plane.) I even called our embassy when I stopped for a layover in Paris, having packed a little red carry-on bag with clothes and toiletries. My suitcase was checked through to Iran, but if I was dissuaded from continuing on, I intended to play *en français* for a few days.

Originally, the itinerary included visits to the ancient cities of Shiraz (called the City of Roses and Poets), the impressive ruins of Persepolis (supposedly burned down by Alexander the Great) and Isfahan (where we looked forward to buying Persian rugs at the bazaar). But almost as soon as we arrived, scheduled events were canceled. Shah Mohammed Reza Pahlavi himself greeted us at a lavish reception that featured hot and cold running caviar. (I bought caviar to take home and was told that I was the only guest who'd paid for it.) But the tenuous stability of the country was immediately apparent. Guards clutching machine guns stood watch even when we walked in the hotel gardens. Bank Melli's fiftieth coincided with my own birthday, on September 12, 1978. Instead of candles on a cake I was treated to a sound-and-light show. Just before returning, I had breakfast with the American ambassador, who commented that he didn't understand the concern about political unrest in the country; the Shah, he contended, was clearly in control. Of course, just four months later, in January 1979, the Shah fled the country he had ruled since 1941. Shortly thereafter, the exiled Muslim leader Ayatollah Khomeini returned from France to form a new government, one that was ardently anti-American.

New York State gave its employees Election Day off, so on Tuesday, November 6, 1979, I was home watching television coverage of the crisis in Iran. Two days earlier, three thousand Iranian militants had seized the U.S. Embassy in Tehran and taken fifty-four staff members hostage. I acted intuitively, like a businessperson, not a lawyer or politician. First I called one of my deputies at home and said, "Send examiners into the four Iranian banks tomorrow morning so we can see every transaction." I asked that all incoming and outgoing telexes be checked every day and that a spreadsheet be produced showing daily assets and liabilities so we could detect any significant fluctuations. The next morning I called Ed Casey, undersecretary at the State Department, and informed him of my intention to monitor any unusual transfers of funds from the Iranian banks. His response was: "There are Iranian banks in New York?"

My move was controversial. "Boss," said the deputy in charge of all commercial banks, "you've got brass boobs." I had informed the State Department because I wanted to confirm that this action would not jeopardize the welfare of the hostages. But the Iranian banks had major credit lines with U.S. banks, and they could have wired all their assets out of the country, leaving us with only their liabilities. Even as the militants held Americans prisoner, Iran maintained an embassy in Washington and paid the bills of Iranian nationals, some of them students, who resided in this country. The plan could have backfired: Iran didn't have to cooperate and could have started an international financial incident by withholding payments from American banks, but the Iranians wanted to remain in good standing in the global financial community.

For a week, we monitored all the money going in and out of the Iranian banks. On November 12 Iran's foreign minister announced publicly that his country intended to withdraw its deposits and those of its government-controlled entities from all American banks. U.S. authorities saw the Iranians' expressed intentions as a prelude to a willful default on Iran's liabilities to U.S. creditors. Two days later, President Jimmy Carter issued Executive Order No. 12170 blocking all official Iranian assets in this country. He was authorized to do so under the International Emergency Economic Powers Act, which granted him the authority to deal with "any unusual and extraordinary threat to the national security, foreign policy or economy of the United States."

Upon learning that the executive order had been signed, I sent full crews of bank examiners into each of the four Iranian banks to ensure compliance. With its assets frozen, Iran agreed to pay for commercial goods already shipped from American companies with fresh money, and we set up channels for funneling $20 million from Tehran to London. There it was turned over to Morgan Guaranty, a New York State–chartered bank, which wired it to an upstate branch of Manufacturers Hanover that was not a member of the Federal Reserve. (Anybody to whom Iran owed money would try to grab it, but we didn't think they would be looking for Iranian money in an obscure Hudson River town.) Manny Hanny wired the money to the Iranian bank in New York, we set up a conduit for sending checks out, and our examiners approved the payments.

It was a highly charged atmosphere. Telegrams arrived from many congressmen and senators whose constituents were Iranian creditors—small-business owners with approved licenses on letters of credit by the U.S. Treasury, who could not get the monies owed to them released. Meanwhile, young Iranian militants were protesting outside the U.S. Embassy in Tehran that we were holding up payments to Iranian students here. In meetings, Bank Melli's manager, Levon D'janece, treated us to a melodramatic outburst. At one point, he charged that the monitoring procedures reflected a lack of confidence in the bank and him personally, that our intention was to close down his bank, and that examiners sent to the bank had been personally abusive to him. Another time he tried to press into my hand a set of keys that opened his bank's doors, saying I might as well run the place. But calmer heads prevailed, and he continued to oversee the paying of bills.

Eventually the Fed took over, but Jimmy Carter's tenure was irrevocably damaged, especially after a secret helicopter mission to rescue the hostages failed spectacularly in April 1980. A blinding desert sandstorm and mechanical problems forced the mission to be scrubbed. Tragically, as the choppers took off to return to their base, one collided with a C-130 transport plane, killing eight American soldiers. The pundits on Wall Street— always first with black humor about global calamities—labeled it Carter's First Annual Desert Classic. He lost his bid for re-election in 1980, and Ronald Reagan reaped the political reward of having the hostages released on his inauguration day, January 20, 1981—444 days after the crisis began. Many Americans watched this joyous homecoming with wet eyes. My tears were especially sweet.

One of my priorities as banking superintendent was encouraging New York banks to invest in the overlooked and unglamorous parts of New York. (Walter Wriston, the Citibank CEO who was known as the world's most influential banker, once came up to me at a meeting of the World Bank and proudly announced, "Madame Superintendent, we just lent Poland fifty million dollars." I said, "How about five million for the Bronx, Walter?")

Oftentimes, when the banking department held hearings about various matters of interest to the public, we'd hear peripherally about "redlining" practices: Banks would discriminate against certain impoverished areas in granting loans for home purchase or improvement. The slightest hint of racial "transition" in a neighborhood could cause mortgage money to dry up. The banks, of course, were shocked—*shocked!*—that such things went on.

In December 1978 the practice was supposedly outlawed by the state legislature (the law passed despite opposition from the Republican senate leadership), and the banking board empowered the S.O.B. to investigate any claims of discrimination. It should be understood how the board operated: The members didn't just go into a small room and decide to adopt some regulation. They agreed to submit an item for comment. They sent notices to financial institutions and anyone else who expressed interest in a particular problem. There was a certain waiting period, usually a month or so, for the interested parties to comment on the proposal in writing. In this way, the board was aware of the views of a wide group of people who wanted to stop redlining.

New banking department regulations designed to combat this offensive practice were based on the federal Community Reinvestment Act of 1977, which had been pushed through Congress by Senator William Proxmire, the Democratic head of the Senate Banking Committee. The new law promised an unprecedented degree of public accountability for lending policies in this country. Banks that wanted to merge, expand or open new branches would be required to define the communities they served and keep detailed information on how they were meeting the credit needs of those communities. Basically, banks would be forced to stop redlining city neighborhoods if they wanted to keep opening branches in the suburbs. Compliance would be taken into account when the banks applied for permits to broaden their activities.

While the law provided sanctions for redlining violations, the practice was hard to pinpoint. Bankers were skilled in explaining how their prohibitively expensive mortgage terms were necessary to minimize risk in an uncertain financial climate. The first transaction to be subject to the new state regulations was the proposed merger between the Brooklyn-based Dime Savings Bank and the Albany-based Mechanics Exchange Savings Bank. Several upstate community groups opposed the merger on the grounds that the Dime had consistently committed redlining, and they feared that the policies of this Goliath (with assets of $4.5 billion) would come to dominate Mechanics (a relative David, with $230 million). While it was the second largest of seven thrift institutions with a branch in downtown Brooklyn, the Dime had granted only seven mortgages in that area—the worst record of all seven banks. About $1 billion, or one fourth of the Dime's total assets, were deposited in its downtown Brooklyn branch, but just over $200,000 in mortgages had been granted in the area the previous year.

Bernard McDermott, a senior vice president at Dime, said

that he thought the bank had done an exemplary job in granting mortgages to deserving individuals. "We consider all of Brooklyn our home base," he declared, "not just downtown." Trying to steer a reasonably sensible course of encouraging mortgage lending without mandating it, I requested that the Dime establish a division of community affairs and reduce the average processing time for approving credit applications to one month. This pleased no one. The bank was angry about being put "on hold," and the New York Public Interest Research Group called me a coward. I always think that when both sides say nasty things about you, it means you're doing a good job.

That spring, the state senate reneged on an agreement to provide $180,000 in enforcement money. This was not politics at its finest. It was Republicans who refused to approve the rather small sum—it was the total allotment for staff salaries, travel, consulting reports and other routine expenses of investigations—because it had been agreed to in the last major political battle fought by former Assembly Speaker Stanley Steingut, the powerful New York Democratic Party boss. Steingut had held up a bill raising the legal interest ceiling on mortgages issued in the

> I always think that when both sides say nasty things about you, it means you're doing a good job.

state until the antiredlining measures were included. The Republicans knew that the bill was good for savings banks, which had all but stopped issuing mortgages. The cost of money to the banks was in the double digits, but they could charge only up to 9.5 percent interest. It was a really tough period: we knew banks could not continue to make loans at interest rates below the cost of money. In April I approved a quarter of a percentage point raise in the mortgage interest ceiling, to 9.75, as allowed by law; rates could rise a quarter of a percent every three months until they reached market level. But the battle against redlining lost its chief advocate, and Steingut's career ended abruptly when he was revealed to be the owner of a chain of nursing homes in deplorable condition.

My fellow Republican, Chairman of the State Senate Banking Committee Jay P. Rolison, Jr., disappointed the community groups when he declared money for watchdogs against redlining unnecessary and suggested a committee to study the problem. (Just what we needed, like the kind of committee that studied whether it would be fiscally responsible for our armed forces to pay six hundred dollars per toilet seat.) It was, said one public interest group, as if the state senate were shilling for the banks. In a supposed compromise, Rolison told his state assembly counterpart, Herman D. Farrell, Jr., that he would accept a budget for checking into individual claims of discrimination but not for investigating bank behavior as part of the application process for expansion. Farrell refused, charging him with deliberately emasculating the new regulations, and managed to add $250,000 for "miscellaneous" expenses to the final banking department budget.

The first time we really bared our teeth about redlining was in June 1980, when we denied an application for a new Nassau County branch of the Jamaica Savings Bank, which left the distinct impression of hostility and arrogance at a public hearing on the subject. Two community groups had asked to meet with bank officials to discuss the region's credit needs, but they were refused. The Jamaica Savings president, Joseph J. Blaine, testified that one group's request was thrown away because it was handwritten, was not on letterhead stationery and was otherwise "unimpressive." Subsequently, the bank refused to meet with any community group representatives who did not have at least one thousand dollars on deposit. "If you truly represent the community," bank chairman Park T. Adikes said loftily, "your members should be our depositors. Bring them in, and we will discuss with them how they want their money to be invested. To have just borrowers dictate where we should put our money is not fair." Adikes called the Community Reinvestment Act "a bad law that is badly administered" and vowed, "None will have more fun challenging it than I will." It was not realistic to expect banks to lose money on mortgages, but it was still a far cry from the nineteenth-century provenance of an institution that prided itself on opening savings accounts for those with no more than a dime to deposit.

In April 1979, a political reporter and columnist named Mark Lieberman wondered in the *Daily News* why the state superintendent of banking was out "promoting herself" with advertising for Muriel Siebert & Co. I asked John J. Marchi, chairman of the State Senate Finance Committee, to send a letter on my behalf to the reporter. "There is a corporate entity bearing her name, to be sure," he wrote. "But if Henry Ford had become banking superintendent after making a go in the automobile business, he probably would not have been expected to change the name of his car." The same subject was revisited on a radio program called "Bull Dog Edition of the *Daily News*." A man named Thomas Poster, claiming to be a close friend of mine, said that he'd had "a few drinks" with me "the other night" at a place frequented by politicians called Christopher's, where I had supposedly said that I was unhappy in my job and would be leaving soon. The last time I'd been at Christopher's was four months before, and I wouldn't have known Thomas Poster if he walked in the room.

I was regularly fending off attacks from the press. In an incredibly misleading 1980 *New York Times* article, Attorney General Bob Abrams criticized the banking department's contracts with private lawyers during my incumbency. In order to hire outside counsel, the department had to receive permission from Abrams' office, the comptroller's office *and* the governor. Each contract had been approved. The banking department did not cost taxpayers one red nickel; by law, regulated institutions were assessed to pay the entire operating cost of the department, including the fees of outside counsel. This we used only in emergencies, such as the imminent failure of a bank, when extensive expert legal resources were required to work virtually round the clock. The article was amazingly mean-spirited, noting that the department had obtained the services of the law firm Hughes, Hubbard & Reed. One of its partners, William A. Volckhausen, was a former banking department employee with whom I remained friends and occasionally had lunch. Yes, in the weeks immediately following the Iranian freeze, I had sought his advice. He had just left the department, and we did not yet have a new general counsel to replace him. I needed help from a senior advisor who knew the Iranian banks from a regulatory standpoint and understood the policy, supervisory and legal issues involved. He was paid the grand sum of $7,300.

Ed Eustace, the deputy superintendent in charge of foreign banks, came with me to the *Times* offices to explain the uniqueness of the Iranian situation. The editors were really quite ethical. Although they would not issue a retraction, they said they'd never had such an understanding of the department before and they "owed" me one. True to their word, the paper repaid its "debt" with a cogent, gratifying article on my tenure when I left the job.

Another *Times* article concerned "aggressive" bank advertising, misleading promotions and the possibility that depositors were not being adequately informed of interest rate yields when opening new accounts. The state banking board had adopted a "Truth in Savings" regulation, which required banks to prepare written statements made available to customers concerning rates and terms for savings and time deposit accounts. The banking department was attacked for ineptitude (quoting an "official" but anonymous source—I assumed it was Bob Morgado, with Governor Carey's blessing). The article left the false impressions that there was a serious consumer abuse problem in the banking industry and that my department wasn't doing its job to correct this problem. The reporter had called from a pay phone at the last minute, asking for a ritual denial, but he never gave us a chance to refute misstatements on the part of the Consumer Affairs Commissioner for New York City, Bruce C. Ratner, who proposed that I coordinate action among bank regulators to ensure that depositors got the best deal. I did not have such authority, and there was such considerable ignorance about which banks came under my jurisdiction that I glibly suggested that Citibank get a state charter if I was to continue to be blamed for its consumer banking policies. Two months after the article appeared, I released a report indicating that all thrifts and the majority of commercial bank offices were complying with the "Truth" regulation. For those few that were still not providing the required written information, bank officials were called in and instructed to take proper action or face penalties.

It seemed I was becoming known for rocking the boat. At one point I was talking with the assistant to State Commerce Secretary John Dyson, with whom I had tangled publicly. "I guess I'm getting a reputation as the bitch of the state agencies," I said. "No," he replied, you're getting a reputation as their conscience." I was disgusted by the paperwork that wasted so much time and realized that the banking department was adding regulations without removing old ones that were no longer applicable. I asked for samples of the reports submitted by banks, check cashers, license lenders and other financial companies, and I was reliably informed by a deputy that half the stuff was filed and never looked at. I invited two representatives of each of the industries regulated by the banking department and asked them for constructive ideas about streamlining the regulation process and reducing the cost burden. I got a rather unenthusiastic response—nobody seemed to think I was serious—but we were able to lower the number of schedules that savings banks had to submit from thirty-nine to thirteen. We developed common application forms for new branches, mergers and trust powers, to be used by both state and federal regulators. We eliminated the necessity for reporting various changes in bank data-processing systems and simplified the reporting and record-keeping requirements relating to crimes against banks.

The disclosures of Bert Lance's banking-related borrowings highlighted the potential for abuse in banker-borrower lending practices. In December 1977 I released a seventy-three-page report recommending the tightening of existing state law, which made it a misdemeanor for bank officials to receive personal loans based on their banks' deposit of funds with other financial institutions. I suggested a periodic review of all correspondent relationships by the boards of directors or executive committees of state-chartered banks. You can imagine how popular this made me with bank officials. And my disrepute was even further guaranteed when I suggested salary cuts for CEOs of banks that were on thin ice fiscally. I couldn't dictate policy, but I had the right to call on any board of directors and say, "Look, this bank has not done well. Why should you pay a bonus to the guy in charge?"

I even got into trouble over my own salary. In November 1980, less than three weeks after facing the voters in the polling booths, the New York State legislature acted in the dead of night to vote itself big fat boosts in "lulus" (bonuses paid to committee chairmen) and give salary hikes to the governor, lieutenant governor, attorney general and more than one hundred other cabinet-level officials, including me. Shortly after the new year, I read in the *Daily News* that 77 percent of the public opposed increases for high state officials. I sent a memo to the man who handled payrolls for the banking department saying that since I had not entered state service for financial gain, I would like to have my state-mandated raise turned back to the state. The bureaucrats were horrified. Apparently the complex bookkeeping entries necessary to deal with such heretofore unknown largesse would cost the state more than the raise. I couldn't simply refuse the money without hopelessly confusing the computer.

There was no prohibition against donating the money. I had

felt enormous appreciation for the city's finest since, several years earlier, I had been held up at gunpoint in the garage of my apartment building by a drug addict who was wanted for killing senior citizens in the Bronx. (Two weeks after this harrowing experience, a New York City policeman killed the mugger during another holdup attempt.) At first I thought my raise should go to the fund to buy bullet-proof vests, but I found out that the city was footing that bill. I checked with the state troopers and found out that *their* vests were paid for by the state, so they didn't need my money either. Eventually, the donation went to the Patrolmen's Benevolent Association. I sent a check for $530 to the PBA's Widows and Orphans Fund every month that I was in office. At least its computers knew how to accept it. I was made an honorary PBA member and given a card with "Muriel" inscribed on a badge. Easily worth the price.

The savings banks of New York State needed saving themselves. It wasn't a matter of bad loans or swindling customers. Many of them were near collapse because of high interest rates. Early in 1980 I started getting calls and letters from presidents of small state-chartered banks telling me that they were reluctantly applying for national charters because of the state usury laws, now woefully out of step with the times. Other states had changed their archaic laws, but New York made it a criminal offense to charge more than 25 percent annual interest on borrowed money, with penalties of up to four years in jail. The banking industry's prime rate—the minimum fee on loans to the largest and most creditworthy companies—was now 19 percent, and charges to lesser borrowers were closing in on the usury ceiling. The law had been meant to discourage loan-sharking, but no one had ever envisioned legitimate loans hitting 25 percent. People were taking their money out of day-of-deposit accounts and putting it in higher-yielding accounts. The thrifts were in trouble for doing what Congress and the regulators told them to do: charge low-interest rates on long-term mortgages. Small rural banks such as Tioga State Bank and Dundee found themselves unable to compete with national banks that operated under lesser constrictions, paying 10, 12, 14 percent interest for their money while still paying current CD rates to keep their deposit customers happy. Some of the thrifts were the object of dirty tactics obviously meant to inflame emotions: one man acting on behalf of Citibank stood outside the Manhattan Savings Bank in Yonkers handing out doll-sized savings passbooks to customers entering and leaving the branch.

In March 1980, a new federal law took effect, giving federally chartered thrifts broad new powers in consumer and business loans, trust operations and other areas. I submitted to the governor a list of recommendations for what the 113 state-chartered thrifts would need to remain competitive. I proposed to the state legislature that our savings banks be given unlimited branching and increased consumer powers to make both secured and unsecured loans, issue credit cards, extend revolving credit, take corporate accounts and make variable-rate and rollover mortgages and second-mortgage loans. This kind of parity was necessary to make the state banks fully competitive with their federally chartered counterparts and to stanch any mass exit of the thrifts from the state system, which would send the entire New York banking system crumbling. When a bank has a federal charter, its priorities are determined by Washington, not by Albany. And when the directives come from Washington, they are not always in the best interests of state residents. The banking board had already lifted one advantage of a federal charter, which was the right to offer free gifts at new branches, opening up a kind of Let's Make a Deal mentality. The newspapers were so cluttered with ads for giveaways of blenders, toasters and TVs that one could almost imagine a power shortage from the communal plugging-in. Consumers were power-mad, storming into banks with pictures of irons that had seven steam vents when they had been given one with only five.

In June I made an all-night lobbying effort at the state legislature to bring to a vote the measures needed for New York thrifts.
All I got out of my efforts was a photograph of me on the front
page of the Sunday *New York Times*, asleep in an armchair at
2:00 A.M. The 1980 legislature, which cheerfully imposed
harsher fines for shooting moose and spent long hours debating
whether "I Love New York" should be stamped on license plates,
recessed without passing the banking bill. The timing was just
terrible: politicians were loath to bring higher interest charges
back to their constituents in an election year.

At the time, under the state constitution, all savings banks
had to be mutual institutions—not public, not private, but
owned by depositors. That law was later changed, so that they
could go public and raise money. By 1981 the Federal Savings
and Loan Insurance Corporation had to provide financial assistance for the mergers of two relatively small federally chartered
thrifts in New York. Our worst-case-scenario projections indi-
cated that ten savings banks, with aggregate deposits of $20 bil-
lion, would become insolvent in 1982. We knew when they
would go broke because their operating losses were coming out
of their net worth, and we knew when that would be exhausted.
(The loans were good and solid, but the banks had to pay out
more in interest to keep the money than they were receiving in
interest coming in.) Many others would find their net worth
declining to such low levels that the financial community would
probably consider them unsafe and unsound. My only recourse
would have been to take possession of the banks when their net
worth was exhausted, declare them insolvent and hold a bidding
contest for the assets, but it would have meant a major run in the
state. About a third of the industry was in imminent danger.

William M. Isaacs, chairman of the Federal Deposit Insurance
Corporation, wanted to merge the failing savings banks into
commercial banks or other financial institutions. I thought it
would be immoral to allow a savings bank to be acquired as a
whole by a commercial bank or nonbanking company, at least as

long as banks were not allowed to compete fully with nonbanks. Thrifts enjoy a community camaraderie that does not exist with larger commercial institutions. People like and trust savings banks. They were a backbone of the housing industry in this country, and the ability of most American families to own a home was the backbone of the nation's economic and political stability. The bank in the most imminent danger of reaching zero assets was Greenwich Savings Bank, and it was my greatest fear that if the FDIC did not handle the situation properly, the headlines would read "Largest Savings Bank Failure in History," and public confidence in the banking system would be severely damaged.

In September, I went to Washington and spent a day in the Rayburn House Office Building, meeting with a half-dozen New York Congressmen. It was a dog-and-pony show—perfunctory sessions scheduled every half hour—but I wanted them to know the grim statistics. In the third quarter of 1981, New York savings banks had suffered a record $372 million loss, and the immediate future was likely to be just as bad—only four of our ninety-nine state-chartered savings banks were expected to report profits for the fourth quarter. (In fact, by the end of the year, New York savings institutions would post aggregate losses of $1.25 billion. Bowery Savings Bank lost more money in 1981 than any U.S. financial institution ever had in a single year—despite banners in its lobbies showing baseball legend Joe DiMaggio saying, "It's a whole new ball game at the Bowery"—and its $114 million deficit was not likely to stand as a record for very long.) I kept making my case that we were one step ahead of the sheriff at many banks, that we'd have to close them and put up a bidding process for their assets. "I can do it once," I said. "I can do it twice. But I cannot do it with a list of banks so big."

Everybody responded pretty much the same way: "New York has archaic laws, and the rest of the country doesn't care." But Governor Carey had appointed a smart young lawyer named Barney Carroll to his Washington office. Feeling as frustrated as I did, he called and said that we should met with Jim Cannon, the administrative assistant to the senate majority leader, Howard Baker, who had worked for Nelson Rockefeller and knew New York. I showed Cannon the list of banks and the dates they would go broke. "Come back next week," he said, "and meet with Senator Baker."

When I arrived for that meeting, Baker was in his office with Senator Jake Garn, Republican head of the Senate Banking Committee. Although New York was in a financial crisis, the thrift industry throughout the country was languishing. Federal law had given S&Ls and savings banks permission to invest in things never before allowed: golf courses, yacht basins—all kinds of nontraditional investments that later blew up. In 1981 the nation's S&Ls and savings banks would lose a staggering $6.4 billion. The failure to push through bank regulatory reform legislation that could ease the woes of the thrifts was generally dropped at Garn's door, although he had tried to reassure the American people about their protection under the Federal Savings and Loan Insurance Corporation.

"There is no doubt about the safety of deposits in our insured financial institutions," he said. "There is absolutely no way the Congress would or will walk away from its commitment to guarantee savings." But he didn't seem to acknowledge the Herculean challenge of safeguarding savers' deposits without depleting the FSLIC's insurance pool. One anonymous regulator interviewed in *Barron's* said of Garn, "He has been a great disappointment, and if you ever say I said it, I'll deny it."

After I had laid bare the banking situation, Senator Baker asked, "Who are you seeing next?" I was going down the hall to the office of Senator William Proxmire, Garn's across-the-aisle counterpart as Democratic head of the Senate Banking Committee. Anytime I had dealt with Proxmire on banking matters, we were always very formal: "Certainly, Ms. Siebert." "Yes, Mr. Senator." As I approached his office, he was standing at the door without his jacket and tie, his shirt open. "Mickie," he said, "I understand we have problems."

"Yes, we do. If something isn't done, the savings banks of New York will shut their doors within a year."

"We can't let that happen," he said.

I was out on my own limb about the thrifts, with no help from the governor's office. I'd written a forty-page report about the problems (the first time I ever sent him something) marked "Confidential" and made four copies: one for Bob Morgado, one for Michael Del Giudice (a Carey associate who later ran Bill Bradley's 2000 presidential campaign), one for the person in Carey's office who followed banking and one for the governor himself. The following day, I was informed that the governor would never read something forty pages long, so I shrank the report to four pages and had it delivered to his home. A few days later, I saw Governor Carey at a party given by his brother in my apartment building. I asked if he had any thoughts about the report and what we could do. "That's a federal problem," he said. "We don't have fifty billion dollars." In other words, since the Federal Savings and Loan Insurance Corporation would be required to bail out the savings banks, he wasn't going to get involved.

In October I flew to Washington to try to convey a sense of emergency. Craig Fuller, Ronald Reagan's assistant for cabinet affairs, got me a brief, ineffective "meet and greet" with the president, who had stated strong opposition to any plan for bailing out the thrift industry. One of the administration's free-market ideologues was quoted as saying, "Nobody ever guaranteed any S&L or its management perpetual bliss." It was the president's own "economic recovery plan," with its tax cuts for individuals, that he thought would spur savings, thus helping thrifts attract fresh funds to make mortgages at the current high rates. But the country was headed into a recession because of double-digit interest rates. Roger Mehle, the assistant secretary of the Treasury who was assigned to look at the problems of New York savings banks, didn't seem to think we had an emergency. He declared that if the banks could meet their outflow—meaning

that if you went to the teller and could withdraw your money—
there wasn't any problem. But under the constitution of New
York State, if the bank was not earning money and the retained
capital was near zero, a sign had to be posted in the window saying that the bank might not be able to pay interest. I called my
friend William Casey, then head of the Central Intelligence
Agency, who helped me get an appointment with Murray Weidenbaum, chairman of the President's Council of Economic
Advisors. If Mehle did not understand the depth of the problem
and take action, Weidenbaum said he'd write a short study and
put it on Ronald Reagan's desk.

To Governor Carey's credit, when he heard that I was running
around Washington asking for help, he left the dais at a luncheon and came to me. "I understand you're fighting for New
York," he said. "Keep up the good work." But the president's
senior policy advisor, a woman named Shannon Fairbanks,
lashed out at me in the press in early November. In a very pissy
statement indicating absolutely no knowledge of my meetings
with Mehle and Fuller, she said it was unfortunate that I had not
fully informed myself of the actions already undertaken by the
White House to deal with the thrift industry crisis. It was only
my utmost determination about preserving public confidence in
the system that prevented me from responding in kind, but I
wrote her a letter detailing my attempts to get White House
attention, during which time no senator, no congressman, no
member of the executive branch had ever suggested that a White
House commission had been established to address these issues.
I didn't hear from Fairbanks, but a few days later I received an
apology from Fuller. "I regret the 'shot over the bow' from our
policy office," he wrote, "and appreciate your courtesy in not
returning the same publicly."

Mehle did write to say that my efforts had persuaded the
banking committee to pass legislation allowing the FDIC to give
us paper for the banks that would shore up their capital position. I requested the New York legislature to amend the state

banking laws, permitting savings banks to recognize capital assistance from the FDIC as a component of their net worth and an authorized source for paying dividends. The minute that happened, starting in November, we merged five thrifts into stronger banks, without inconveniencing any customers. Each of the banks closed under one name and opened the next morning under a new name, losing their identities but keeping their assets. We established a mechanism and a standard for merging a diminished bank into a healthy one, and I was proud we were able to do it. One of the failing thrifts, the New York Bank for Savings, had been the first to be chartered in New York; it had survived the Civil War and the Depression, but it couldn't survive the current inflation, and it was merged out of existence on its 163rd birthday.

Even *The New York Times* acknowledged that not since the Great Depression had a banking superintendent dealt with so many critical problems. I was a political neophyte when I started, and it would have made my life a lot easier at the outset if somebody had given me a two-day course explaining who was who and why in state government. I knew nothing about the legislature and its protocol, about schmoozing and glad-handing. I didn't know that if I called on Warren Anderson, the majority leader of the state senate, I should also call on the minority leader, Stanley Steingut. Nor did I understand the deep-rooted upstate-versus-downstate antagonism that led someone to ask me, in the middle of the Hong-Shang mess, "Why are you worried about those apple growers upstate?" I didn't understand about political patronage or about certain areas of government that had become dumping grounds for people who weren't qualified but needed jobs and held unofficial IOUs. In many cases, I hired people with no relevant experience because I made a deal with the governor's office: I would take one of theirs if I could go out and hire a top person for a key opening. Bob Morgado would call and say, "Look, you've got an opening, and I've got some people." But it would have been nice if there had been more exempt spots.

I spent more time as S.O.B. than a dozen predecessors in the job, and not one New York bank failed during my tenure, despite nationwide bank failures. I was called the most powerful woman in New York for five years, but it wasn't hard to stay humble. The New School for Social Research announced in its catalog that there would be a lecture by Muriel Siebert, the first woman to hold the position of superintendent of baking.

6

A GUEST AT THE GRAND OLD PARTY

Lead, follow or get the hell out of the way.

I happen to be a bleeding-heart Republican: fiscally conservative, strong on defense and tough on crime, but concerned about the ease of purchasing guns and passionately prochoice. I believe abortion is a sad and serious decision that every woman must be allowed to make for herself relying on her own conscience and her doctor. Nobody celebrates abortion. But women have always found, and always will find, ways to protect their reproductive freedom. The only questions remain: Will it be safe and legal? And will it be limited to the wealthy? When you live in New York City, you see the worst part of the welfare system, which should be treated as a response to a temporary emergency, not a permanent way of life. The crisis of unwanted children guarantees generations of people for whom public assistance is a family legacy. "Right to life" has come to mean "right to birth." Children need love, shelter, food and education. If the antichoice people want to force women to carry and bear children, then there must be people who will cherish these children and donate money for their necessities. Otherwise, the odds are that they will never be productive citizens.

Even before I joined the Stock Exchange, and certainly afterward, I was smoked out for government jobs by administrations in both parties. I was impressed with the way Richard Nixon opened up trade in China—a potentially huge market—with his historic trip to Beijing in 1972. When he sent me a pen set com-

memorating his first inauguration, I sent him a pen set com-
memorating my NYSE membership. I was interviewed and
basically offered the position of Civil Aeronautics Board commissioner. I refused it because when I asked how I would spend
my day, I was told, "The staff does the work and makes a rec-
comendation and you vote it." When Ronald Reagan won the
1980 presidential election, I was interviewed to be Treasurer of
the United States. I had a lawyer study the Constitution in prepa-
ration for the meeting and realized it was not a real job—the
Treasurer essentially signs the dollar bills and promotes savings
bonds. It's always been "the woman's job," and over the years
I've told two or three presidents that they ought to give it some
real duties. During the Carter administration, I was asked to
consider the Federal Aviation Agency. But I'd made a decision
that unless it was a real policy-making position, what did I need
it for? The positions under consideration were usually those of
assistant, rather than head of a department or agency, and I
found the idea of being second-in-command unappealing. I'm
willing to live with my own mistakes, but I don't want to live
with anyone else's.

My stint with the banking department convinced me that
many financial laws needed changing, and I thought I knew
more about the issues than a lot of people in Congress. There
were too many lawyers in Washington—the country needed help
from people who knew how to run businesses—and the Senate
could certainly use some sisterhood for its lone woman, Nancy
Kassebaum of Kansas. I had discovered how restrictive the role

---

I'm willing to live with my own mistakes, but I don't want to live with anyone else's.

---

of regulator can be and how creative the role of legislator can
be. Plus, I *hated* New York's senior senator, Daniel Patrick
Moynihan. When the New York savings banks were going under
and I went to Washington for help, he didn't lift a finger. In fact,

he told me to go down the hall and speak to my Republicans.

By 1982 there was a certain confluence of events in my life: Governor Carey had made the surprising announcement that he would not seek re-election that fall, ostensibly resenting the invasion of his private life and wanting to increase his net worth before retiring by working in the private sector. Lieutenant Governor Mario Cuomo, who hoped to replace him in November, said that I could remain in my job if his administration took over in Albany. I no longer had the fiscal responsibility of supporting an aging parent. I had been away from the stock market for almost five years and considered selling my firm to stay in public service. (It had not done well in the blind trust. In fact, the only reason it had stayed alive was the growth of the industry.) I saw politics work beautifully with the savings bank bailout package, although I grew increasingly frustrated with bureaucratic red tape and temporary stopgap measures. I had spent more than twenty years on Wall Street, where the penalty for fuzzy thinking is swift and painful. I couldn't understand how government operated in such a fog, with such circular reasoning.

Then in March the leading Republican hopeful to face Moynihan was forced to withdraw from the race after he was caught lying about his military background. The former U.S. Representative Bruce F. Caputo made false claims about being an army lieutenant during the Vietnam War, then outraged veterans by calling these misstatements "bar talk." With newspapers reporting on Caputo's "delusions of military service," Moynihan smugly told reporters that he would run unopposed if the Republicans insisted, but that he'd prefer a formidable candidate.

Remember the name Melvin Klenetsky? Of course you don't. He had run unsuccessfully against New York City Mayor Edward I. Koch the year before and was the only Democrat challenging Moynihan. Since Klenetsky's candidacy seemed to consist of rants about a conspiracy of London bankers and stuffed Eskimos in the American Museum of Natural History, few people took him seriously. Moynihan just ignored him. If I wanted to make a serious commitment to public service, the time was ripe. Lead, follow or get the hell out of the way. I sent preliminary letters to New York's sixty-two Republican county chairmen and got enough encouraging words to go forward. But first I had to arrange a "responsible termination" from the banking department. Government is not like business; you don't just walk in on a Friday and say, "I quit." That was when Morgado, with whom I had come to a grudging understanding, told me that I didn't have to quit; I could take a leave of absence. It was a satisfying conclusion to a bumpy ride.

Many prospective Republican candidates had shied away from the race when it appeared that Caputo was a lock, but the field quickly became crowded with latecomers. Rudolph Giuliani, then the U. S. deputy attorney general, was considering a run, encouraged by the incumbent, Senator Alfonse M. D'Amato. Ronald Lauder, ambassador to Austria and scion of the Estée Lauder cosmetics fortune, was seeking campaign finances. Whitney North Seymour, Jr., a former state senator and U.S. attorney, had already announced his candidacy, his first political bid since losing a congressional race to Ed Koch twelve years earlier. A six-foot-six patrician known as "Mike" (pundits joked that he had three last names), Seymour was urged into the race by a group of Rockefeller-era Republicans who were concerned about the national GOP's drift to the right. Two other hats in the ring belonged to Henry Diamond, a former state environmental conservation commissioner, and Jacqueline Minor, a former history instructor at an upstate community college, married to a federal judge.

The morning that I announced my candidacy, at a press conference in the elegant drawing room of the Helmsley Palace Hotel, began inauspiciously. The car that was supposed to pick me up was late, and a large wall banner with my name didn't arrive on time, so the walnut paneling behind me was festooned with helium balloons, making it look like a children's party. I had to stand on a milk carton in my stocking feet to see over the lectern. But the state Republican chairman, George Clark, Jr., stood beside me and said that more than 60 percent of the GOP county leaders were backing me. When it was my turn to speak, I talked about the sluggish economy. We had double-digit inflation, stratospheric interest rates, a $1 trillion federal budget deficit on which *the interest alone* was more than $1 billion. The war in Vietnam had never been paid for, and when bonds for that cost came due, they would be at double or even triple the original interest rate. The United States was like a family living beyond its means. I promised that I was willing and able to make the hard budget choices needed to cure the nation's economic ills. Recovery would take leaner and tougher management, more productive labor and both local and state cooperation in offering business incentives. I was a director ex officio of several state agencies and had watched talented scientists move to other states. I wanted to reverse the loss of jobs and business to the Sun Belt with tax exemptions, low-cost loans and an emphasis on new technologies.

There were a few incidents of blatant sexism. One of the county chairmen asked how I would feel if I didn't get a chance to be on the ballot. I answered that naturally I'd be very disappointed. "Aren't you going to be a bitch like other women?" he asked. Another remarked, "I guess it's about time we had a broad on the ticket," then asked parenthetically, "You don't mind if I call you a broad, do you?" I needed his support, so I just smiled.

Admittedly, I was an odd fit for the Grand Old Party, but Republicans in New York reminded me of the Republicans in Ohio, where I grew up—conservative fiscally and moderate socially. I have always believed that when someone really needs help, it is government's obligation to assist, but welfare should not become a way of life. I supported the Equal Rights Amendment. I defended President Reagan's tax bill (along with Democratic House Speaker Tip O'Neill, among others) but had reservations about his approach to economic recovery. I thought that a tax cut would get the economy going, but there were all kinds of ways to provide the government with the greater revenues it needed to solve its problems.

I got into trouble when I started broaching ideas. I had read a study about taxing the "underground economy"—that is, cash businesses that escaped the IRS—as a means of eliminating the deficit, and I thought the idea merited further research. But it was misinterpreted as picking on waiters and cab drivers. Street crime in New York had reached alarming records—there was a rash of gold-chain snatchings on the subways that was almost directly attributable to drug addicts desperate for the money to buy their next fix. I'd had the terrifying experience of being robbed by an addict who "specialized" in parking garages with only one attendant, and the look in his eyes when he had me locked in the bathroom of my building's garage was that of somebody who would stop at nothing to get at my purse. The British were allowing addicts to register for a monthly supply of narcotics at a drugstore, and they weren't plagued by our kind of street crime. Late one night I'd gone to the branch of the popular Boots Chemists in London's Piccadilly Circus and watched the addicts standing in line to get their monthly allotment at midnight. When I saw that the British approach looked civilized, I said we should study it here and raised the possibility that taxes could be collected on legal sales. Studying something and advocating it are two different things, but the conservatives later did a number on me for it.

I certainly didn't adhere to rigid partisan dogma, but nothing was more controversial than my stance on reproductive freedom. I tried to make the Republican power structure more sensitive to the real hopes and dreams of women. It didn't take a genius to understand why, in the latest Gallup Polls, women had a considerably lower opinion of President Reagan than men did. Women who represented the GOP had as much to do with its leadership as a mannequin had to do with running Bloomingdale's department store. In my opinion, women have not reached the top rung—where they are as deeply involved in policy as men—in *either* party.

Although Carey had decided not to run for re-election—the first time since 1954 that an incumbent governor wasn't in the race—the GOP had no single "heir apparent." Lewis E. Lehrman, who had made a fortune in the Rite Aid drugstore chain, was accused of trying to buy votes with a slick, expensive media blitz, frequently wearing his trademark red suspenders and rolled-up shirtsleeves. He'd never held elected office and alienated many party regulars by announcing, "I am going to be the first governor since 1923 who has come from west of the Catskills"—a claim he justified because his family had established drugstores in the suburbs. Demonstrating upstate credentials was a common theme for political hopefuls that year, including the two Democrats who wanted to occupy the Executive Mansion in Albany: Ed Koch gave an interview to *Playboy* magazine in which he disparaged life outside the big city. Perhaps to atone, he went around talking about the number of horses stabled on Staten Island so often, it was said that many reporters could lip-synch the story. Lieutenant Governor Cuomo was obviously hoping for more Koch *faux pas* when he called on the mayor to release the other thirteen and half hours of interview tapes and invoked his own tenure as the host of a Rochester radio talk show.

I rented two rooms on the top floor of a Manhattan brownstone owned by a friend and hired Nixon's former office manager and Ronald Reagan's former campaign manager. I didn't think I could do a good job representing New Yorkers if I didn't listen to what they had to say, and I promised to open district offices in five upstate cities—Buffalo, Binghamton, Rochester, Syracuse and Albany—all with toll-free phone numbers. Because regional offices were allocated based on population, Moynihan could have had a presence in all those upstate cities too, but he had only two. (One of them was in the county where he lived, and voters had to use their own dimes to call.) As I went out speaking to local political chapters, I'd always start by saying, "We are burying our country under a mountain of debt"—a personal rendition of the familiar electronic billboard in Times Square that continually calculates each citizen's share of the astronomical national liability. People would come to these meetings and pay fifteen dollars for all the food they could eat. As I was being introduced, I'd be looking at faces buried in their plates. But the moment I mentioned the mountain of debt, their faces would come out of their food.

My campaign trail was uneventful. The only scandal the opposition could drum up, about a week before the June nominating convention, was the revelation that I had once contributed $150 to Moynihan's Senate campaign. (I didn't remember it, but Moynihan's treasurer had been a friend of mine for twenty years, and I figured he probably just palmed a ticket off on me. Mike Seymour's father had also written Moynihan a check.) But there was controversy in Nassau County, which was a critical battleground. Two years earlier, in the 1980 Republican primary, that area of Long Island had produced more votes than the five heavily populated boroughs of New York City and had provided Al D'Amato with his margin of victory over four-term incumbent Jacob K. Javits; this time it was still expected to produce the greatest single block of votes in the state. The Nassau Republican organization was the most effective in New York State—arguably the most potent grassroots political group in the nation—and it was behind me. But the chairman, Joseph M. Margiotta, had just been convicted of one count of mail fraud and five counts of extortion, having secured a commitment to share with friends the commissions of Nassau County's official insurance broker. (At his trial, Margiotta admitted that if the broker had refused to share the goodies, he "probably" would have stripped him of his reward.)

Margiotta's fellow politicians claimed that their leader had gotten a bum rap for practicing politics as usual, that he was simply engaged in political patronage, which means rewarding friends, just as his predecessors had done. Soon after he was sentenced to two years in prison, the Executive Committee of the Nassau County Republican Party voted unanimously to amend party rules that automatically removed convicted felons from office. The county Board of Elections declared that since Margiotta was appealing to a higher court, his conviction was really a suspended sentence. Mike Seymour refused to attend the annual Nassau Republican dinner for the party faithful, citing a previously scheduled speaking engagement, but when asked if he would have gone had his calendar been clear, he said, "I think I'll hide behind Harry Truman's rule not to answer a hypothetical question." I went to the dinner and shared a dais with Margiotta. He was still the county chairman and had been unfailingly polite and decent to me; plus, he had the biggest block of delegates, and his case was under appeal.

Less than two weeks before the state convention, a widowed Brooklyn assemblywoman named Florence Sullivan entered the race. Her Bay Ridge district had been eliminated during reapportionment, leaving her with little chance of reelection. (Ironically, when she returned to law school after raising a family, one of her teachers was Mario Cuomo.) Although our gender probably linked us in some people's minds, it was hard to find common ground in style and substance, even on the so-called "women's issues" that inevitably shaped the campaign. Sullivan defended virtually all of Reagan's major initiatives, including his economic programs and plans for a defense buildup—seemingly myopic about large tax cuts and spending increases leading ineluctably to the federal deficit. She insisted that a nuclear arms freeze would be "very disadvantageous" to the country and declared herself ardently antiabortion, *especially* when it involved Medicaid funding. This would disproportionately penalize poor women. Although I personally favored a policy that made terminating an unwanted pregnancy safely available to *all* women, I realized that it was a sensitive issue. I considered adding a box to the federal income tax forms, indicating whether or not someone's taxes should support government-funded abortions—like the box that gives an individual a choice to make a presidential campaign contribution.

The Conservative Party announced that Sullivan was the only acceptable contender, then set about getting her elected by any means available. But up until the last moments of the state convention in June, the Conservatives tried to get me to change my position on abortion. Members of their coalition visited me in my New York Sheraton suite at midnight. "Just say you're anti-choice for now," I was told, "and there won't be a primary. You can change your opinion in two or three days." But if I had to lie to get the nomination, why run for office?

The Republican convention (technically, only a meeting of the state committee for nominating purposes) turned into a contentious three days of maneuvering, cajoling, threatening and shouting. On the first ballot, Seymour won two thirds of the vote; I got one third, guaranteeing the first primary in New York GOP history the following September. But Lew Lehrman's people, on orders from the Conservatives (who would announce him as their party's gubernatorial candidate a few days later), passed the word to their delegates to give Sullivan enough votes on the second ballot to keep her in the race. You could actually hear the words "How many do you need?" being asked of people like the Brooklyn party leader Fred Pantaleone, who was roaming the floor looking for Sullivan votes. By the third and final roll call, I'd held on to my third of the votes, while Sullivan dropped to a mere 3 percent of the total, and the state committee announced Seymour as favorite son.

Lehrman won a two-thirds majority for the gubernatorial nomination, but that was not enough to offset a primary challenge by Paul Curran, a fair-minded but rather colorless former federal prosecutor and party stalwart, whose father had been the longtime GOP chairman in Manhattan. (Curran was promoted by the entrenched party bosses, who seemed to fear a takeover of the party by a wealthy outsider, as had happened before with Rockefeller. One political pundit wrote that Curran's main qualification for the job was that he wasn't Lehrman.) Ronald Reagan, in town to address a disarmament conference at the United Nations, stopped by at the official close of convention business. He urged everyone to fight cleanly and play nicely among themselves, citing the "Eleventh Commandment"—a chestnut from his presidential campaign: *Thou shalt not speak ill of another Republican.* Perhaps he was also there in penance for his off-the-cuff remark some months earlier that Ed Koch would make a good governor. His presence dispossessed Party Chairman Clark from the presidential suite and stole the thunder from many delegates and committee workers who were denied admission to a cocktail party. Under heavy security, the president posed for photo ops with everyone who had qualified for the primary and promised not to endorse any of the unresolved candidacies, saying, "I know I have to be neutral."

It was a summer of spirited primary campaigning. Seymour attacked Moynihan on a variety of issues (like the senator's pledging not to use a new tax break for lawmakers, yet still charging personal expenses to his campaign). I said little against the senator, instead stressing my own experience, although I did mention that out of one hundred senators in the Senate, only nine had poorer attendance records.

The names Seymour, Sullivan and Siebert did not exactly dominate the headlines that summer. None of us had enough money for a TV ad campaign, but any television advertising would likely have been eclipsed by the media blitzes launched by both the Republican and Democratic candidates for governor. Their hard-fought, big-money races allowed little chance for voters to know the candidates trying to unseat Moynihan. When I campaigned at the New York State Fair upstate, the first two questions from a puzzled wire-service reporter were "Who are you running against?" and "When is the primary?" Things got so bad that one upstate newspaper ran head shots of all three of us on the front page over the headline: WHO ARE THESE PEOPLE? Seymour had to get himself arrested for disorderly conduct to draw any real attention (he violated a ban on leafleting at a county fair near Albany).

I drew some flak when I accused my party's gubernatorial candidate of trying to buy the election with his bottomless coffers. I was further criticized when my financial statements were released, revealing a 1981 IRS return with eighteen tax shelters listed. These were all small and quite legal. (I always said that the only way I could cheat on taxes was to take friends out for dinner and claim it as a business expense—and most of them *did* become clients.) Some of the shelters involved federally funded (FHA and HUD) housing for poor people, which at least had a more altruistic connotation. Some involved oil—less humanitarian, but if you hit a dry hole, you've lost your entire investment. I've got a few dry holes to show for my investments. But I received the most attention for my trip to the Middle East.

I felt quite comfortable talking about the economy, such as plans for a $1,000 income tax credit to anyone who bought an American-made car that got at least twenty-five miles per gallon. But, wanting to bolster my understanding of foreign policy, I made plans to visit Israel and Lebanon, clearing the trip with the State Department and making arrangements with the Israeli consul general here. New York political hopefuls often took three *I* trips—to Israel, Italy and Ireland—to dramatize their interest in the heritage of the predominant hometown voters. I was accused of pandering and grandstanding, but frankly, the trip could have had the opposite result, since the primary Republican constituency is not Jewish.

I made an appointment to see the head of the central Israeli bank when I arrived (as S.O.B., I regulated the Israeli banks in New York), but he took one look at the itinerary planned for me and said, "They've got you sitting by hotel pools too much, like a typical politician. This is a trip for someone who just wants to get credit for having come here." With one phone call, he made

changes. I was not permitted to visit West Beirut, the center of
the conflict, occupied by the Palestine Liberation Organization
(though there was a cease-fire in effect after President Reagan
called on Israeli Prime Minister Menachem Begin to stop bombing). But I traveled by jeep on the front lines with armed military
escorts and viewed the PLO stronghold from a schoolhouse set
up as a control point. Within the next year, these headquarters
would be bombed, and two people I met would be killed.

I had never witnessed the horrors of war firsthand, and when
rockets went off over my head, at first I thought it was thunder. I
was warned not to touch anything or go astray, because I could
run into mines or booby traps. At one point I had to crawl on
hands and knees; I was told that if my head was visible, I might
be shot. Israel was trying to secure a twenty-five-mile buffer zone
along the Lebanese border, but the price was enormous civil-
ian bloodshed and devastation. I saw surface-to-air missiles,
bumper-to-bumper nighttime convoys of supply trucks, a field
hospital with tanks guarding each door. I saw leveled towns,
buildings in ruin, people living in rubble with no lights or water.
A scheduled meeting with the prime minister was canceled
because of the previous week's sensitive negotiations over a new
cease-fire. I came away supporting continued arms sales to
Israel, even though some officials believed that the Israelis had
failed to abide by agreements restricting U.S. arms use to defen-
sive actions. I also came away believing that Israel should have
mounted a full-scale attack on Beirut at the beginning of the
siege or else have stayed out. Even a PLO withdrawal would not
end the conflict.

Florence Sullivan got attention as a spoiler: A Republican-
Conservative split would further fracture a coalition that, just
two years before, had helped propel Al D'Amato to the Senate
over Jacob Javits—running on the Liberal ticket after having
lost the GOP primary—and Democrat Elizabeth Holtzman.

Sullivan, a captive of the right wing, tried to paint both Seymour and me into the same ideological corner as Moynihan, lambasting Seymour's opposition to school prayer and my support of Medicaid-funded abortions. She attacked me as a GOP defector because I had served in the administration of a Democratic governor, calling me "a feisty little thing" and saying "You wouldn't want her for an enemy." She was furious when I pointed out that *she* was the one who had refused to sign the Republican loyalty oath to support the primary winner. New York is one of the few states where you can run on two or three political tickets at the same time. She was the candidate for the Conservative and Right to Life parties while she was running in the Republican primary.

Two days before the November election, a pro-Sullivan flyer arrived in the mail. I was startled to see that it bore the same mailing label as a piece of pro-Lehrman propaganda that had arrived earlier, with the same misspellings and punctuation. The Conservative Party, I would later learn, had paid for printing and mailing 360,000 pieces of literature for Sullivan and had allowed her campaign to use its nonprofit discount postal privileges (four to five cents each, rather than the usual eleven cents for bulk mailing at the time). Under New York State law, any citizen can look through county records to see who voted (although not how a vote was cast) in the primary and/or general election. Lehrman had his representatives examine the records of sixty-two counties and create mailing labels; his campaign then gave duplicate copies of the labels to the Sullivan campaign for her flyer, which labeled me a "baby killer." And it was timed at the eleventh hour to preclude a response.

The customary Tuesday election was shifted to a Thursday to accommodate both the Jewish New Year and a delay in Justice Department approval of legislative district lines. That Tuesday, on my way back from temple, I was told that the *New York Post* had released the results of a poll showing that I was ahead, with 17 percent of the vote, compared to 9 percent for Seymour and 6 percent for Sullivan. There were 68 percent still undecided, but the pollsters announced, "All signs point to a Siebert victory." The paper endorsed Sullivan, without bothering to mention that her politics would deny an abortion to a twelve-year-old who had been raped by her stepfather.

Somehow the voters of New York never got the memo about my assured victory. And what the paper also failed to mention was the fact that primaries tap a different group of voters than a general election. The extremes come out: the extreme right of the Republican Party and the extreme liberals on the Democratic line. I waited in a suite of the hotel that the Republican Party had staked out for most of the candidates with a small group of friends, the room draped with triumphal banners and balloons. But there was no victory—just an increasing sense of frustration and silence as we saw the numbers come in for Sullivan. She won the primary. Seymour and I split the vote of the moderates. On November 2, Sullivan lost the senate election to Moynihan by a huge margin.

Good Republican that I was, I had voted for Lehrman. But I called him after his narrow loss to Mario Cuomo. "I've got those labels," I said, "and if you ever run for office again, I'll take out a full-page ad and display them." He slammed down the phone. Mike Seymour was a man of principle—back in the days of Watergate, when he was convinced that his boss, Attorney General John Mitchell, was a crook, he dared to prosecute. After the general election, he and I joined forces to sue the Conservative Party. We took our case all the way to the Supreme Court, which declined to hear it but directed us to file a complaint with the Federal Elections Commission. After eight (count 'em, eight) years, the Conservative Party signed a civil consent order admitting that it had violated federal law by making an excessive contribution to Sullivan and failing to report it. The fine was fifteen thousand dollars (as testament to the Conservatives' shoestring operation, it was paid in installments), and the headline in *The New York Times* said, GOP LOSERS WIN THEIR CASE.

There was a bit of divine justice in the election results: If

Lehrman had not given Sullivan those mailing labels and I had been on the ticket, I might not have won, but I might have pulled enough votes for Lehrman to edge out Cuomo.

Several months later, I sent a letter to President Reagan, knowing that in all likelihood it would never reach him. "The Gender Gap is real and justified," I wrote. "For the first time in thirty years of voting, I have a deep conflict between being a woman and voting Republican. I do not believe your close advisors are sensitive enough to today's women and their very legitimate concerns." I got a response from Frederick J. Ryan, Jr., director of presidential appointments and scheduling. "Unfortunately," he wrote, "the President's calendar is particularly heavy and demanding at this time, and an opportunity is not foreseen when an appointment could be scheduled." I wrote the same sort of letter to President George Bush almost ten years later. His response? "Rest assured that I respect and am grateful for the role that women are playing in the success of the Republican Party."

It's important to have people going from business to government—they bring a fiduciary point of view. But it's almost impossible for good candidates who don't have money, and it's embarrassing to stand in a room asking people for money, knowing full well that after the election, the same people will be back asking for favors. Way too much money and time are spent in the futile argument about whether the government has any right to be in our bedrooms. A few years after the election, I joined the New York State Republican Family Committee, a group of three hundred prochoice lawyers, doctors, businesspeople and civic leaders, predominantly women, all of whom believed that reproductive choice issues should not be in the party platform and that government should not be meddling in their lives. But twenty years after my election loss, the same debate still divides the Republican Party, and still changes the outcome of some elections.

7

RATE WAR IS HELL

Make the customer whole.

I blew $400,000 on the Senate primary. I don't have that many $100,000 bills to waste, so I had to get back to the business of making money. But in January 1983, like Rip Van Winkle waking up after a long sleep, I returned to a firm in shambles. Mine. Under the blind trust, I'd been allowed monthly statements while I was at Banking, and I knew that the firm wasn't doing well. I knew it in anecdotal ways, too: At my yearly physical, my doctor's wife, who was also his nurse, asked, "Doesn't your firm wish to do business with me anymore? My stocks were sent back to me."

Siebert & Co. had always cleared through another brokerage on a "fully disclosed" basis. That meant the clearing firm sent statements and bills to individual clients, carried the actual stock certificates (either physical or electronic) and held the overall fiscal responsibility for the account. (The other type of arrangement is known as "omnibus," in which the transactions of multiple accounts are combined and the identities of individual account holders are not revealed.) When I left my company, the clearing firm was a subsidiary of Merrill Lynch called Broadcorp. Many discounters had started to clear through large traditional brokerages, and some Wall Street seers saw this as the surreptitious incursion of discount boutiques that the major houses had refused to establish internally. At the time Broadcorp had the maximum insurance of $2.5 million on each account. (Accounts are now protected in their entirety at most solid brokerages, all of which contribute to the Securities Investor Protection Corporation.)

But when I got back, the firm was clearing through Purcell, Graham & Co., which had only the minimum required insurance of $500,000 per account. Big accounts had left because, since the accounts were larger than the insurance, they didn't feel secure—rightly so, as it turned out: Purcell, Graham was subsequently censured and fined by the NYSE. And the new clearing firm couldn't handle the volume when the market was running. In some cases, it was sending out two invoices, or two checks, or somebody else's check. I received other calls from people claiming that Siebert & Co. was "kiting" their money—that is, making it extremely difficult to get cash from their accounts. Dividends from *my* regular account were not sent as they should have been, and if other accounts were receiving the same service, it was a miracle that the firm had any customers left. Our previous accountants had been replaced too, by a small firm, probably because it was cheaper. Small firms can be excellent, but they have to schedule their work. I asked for a mini-audit and couldn't be accommodated because the office didn't have enough people. So I switched accountants immediately.

Shortly after I returned, I got an offer to sell the firm to a large bank for $2 million. That did not include the Stock Exchange seat. We didn't have much book value, but we had licenses in almost every state. My apartment and weekend home were paid up. If I had taken that money, I could have run for public office again and still had enough income from stocks and bonds for financial security. And I might have done just that if things had been different on Wall Street. But I felt a sense of obligation as a role model. I had been a member of the Stock Exchange for fifteen years. For the first ten years, it was 1,365 men and little ol' me, and there was still no other woman-owned firm of any size that owned a seat. When you are a role model, there are times when you do what you don't want to do, and times when you don't do what you want to do. Plus, I *liked* the Street, and I liked

having a *private* private life. When I went to the banking department, I had put my Mercedes in storage and bought a little
Volkswagen convertible, thinking that it would be unseemly for
a public servant to go tooling around in such an ostentatious car.
When I ran for office I realized I couldn't drive a German car in
parts of the state with high unemployment, so I traded it in for a

---

**When you are a role model, there are times when
you do what you don't want to do, and times
when you don't do what you want to do.**

Chrysler. I'd also bought some polyester knit suits and was told
not to wear pants too often. The day I arrived back on Wall Street,
I pulled my Mercedes into the garage wearing a suede pantsuit.
Nobody could grouse, "There go my tax dollars at work."

At my firm there wasn't a single person still working who
had been there when I'd left, including the person running the
show. The blind trust responsible for selecting a chief operating
officer in my absence had chosen a woman named Rita Malm,
who came from the bond part of Wall Street. The company had
moved to a new building, and she was installed in an office
with a marble bathroom and shower. On my first day back, she
said to me, "Don't use that—it's *my* bathroom," so I had a
pretty good idea that it wasn't going to work. During that first
week back, a reporter called to talk about my return; Rita
thought that *she* should be handling the interview. The next
day she announced, "This firm is only big enough for one of
us"—then presented me with her version of "an equitable separation formula." This included a month of vacation pay, ten
weeks of separation pay and escrow incentive pay. She thought
she had provided the firm with services that would earn a certain amount of money in the future; accordingly, she wanted
me to put that amount in escrow so she'd get a bonus if the
extra business came through.

Now that I was back behind the wheel, there was one driving motivation: Make the customer whole. So many complaints came in about calls not being answered or returned that I had "Siebert dollars" printed, giving justified complainants a discount on future trades. It was good business: Bringing in each customer cost thirty to forty dollars in advertising, so it paid not to let them run out the door. We mailed announcements to more than fifty thousand people, hoping that old accounts would give us another try.

Make the customer whole.

I knew we had to be as polite and error-proof as possible. When the discount business was started, all that was necessary to be successful was advertising and a fair execution. Rudeness was tolerated because the founders were mavericks. "Rock 'em and sock 'em" was acceptable to those investors who were interested only in saving money. Now I knew it was time for setting some new rules. I couldn't sanction my name and accomplishments bringing in business, only to see customers lost and my reputation damaged. Employees were sent the following directives:

- *Please answer the phone: "Muriel Siebert and Company. . . . _____ speaking."*
- *Avoid shifting calls to customer service, where calls get lost and customers get annoyed.*
- *Only three days of paid sick leave. After that, you need a doctor's note.*
- *Tuesday inspection. Work areas to be neat, clean and orderly.*
- *Dress appropriately. Customers expect propriety from people dealing with their money.*
- *If you walk by a phone that is ringing, try answering it. It's probably not for you, but this business makes money when phones are answered.*
- *I realize that many customers are irritating, but I expect and*

demand that every Siebert employee be courteous and not short-tempered.
• *EVERYONE MUST BE CALLED BACK.*

The time that I'd been away was one of most volatile and turbulent periods in Wall Street history, characterized by landmark mergers and revolutionary products such as CMOs, or collateralized mortgage obligations, which are mortgages packaged as bonds for resale but separated into different classes with different dates when payment comes due. Other new products were derivatives like futures and options, the characteristics and value of which depend on their underlying securities. There also had been a paradigm shift in emphasis from strictly equities to financial services. I was coming back to something highly competitive. A lot of firms that hadn't been in existence five years before were now several times our size. By going to the banking department just as the discount brokerage business was taking off, I had missed five important years of growth, and I had to relearn the industry. In the olden days, every order had had to be executed by a member of the Stock Exchange, but electronics were now playing an important role in our business. It used to be that we'd get an order and call or wire it down to the floor of the Exchange. There a clerk would give it to a member of the firm or a two-dollar broker, who in turn would execute the order or put it on the specialist books as a limited order. Now we were taking and inputting orders with an electronic delivery system called Direct Order Turnaround, or DOT, which confirmed a buy or sell order within one or two minutes at a fraction of the cost. This rapid-response system was hailed as a democratic leap forward from the days when information was disseminated slowly through the pecking order of the investment community—with the little guy coming last.

One of the ways Siebert & Co. was behind was that it was just about the only discount firm where the phone calls weren't taped. When I started in the business, we never had anything in writing. Your word was your bond. I did multimillion-dollar deals on the phone without so much as a handshake. If you broke your word and reneged on a trade, people wouldn't talk to you again, let alone do business with you. When we started in the discount business, I used to have customers who would send me a box of candy with a thank-you note that said, "Ms. Siebert, I sold three hundred shares of IBM through you, and I saved so much on the trade that I was able to take my family away for the weekend." The business is much more impersonal now that so much trading is done electronically, and we don't really know most of our clients. It's not like having a salesman bringing in Mr. and Mrs. Smith. In some cases, we don't have any personal or even voice contact with customers who are trading exclusively on-line.

I hired Bob Gray, the public relations expert who had been one of the Lockheed lobbyists and then Ronald Reagan's appointments secretary in the White House. I paid his firm a monthly retainer of $2,500 plus "manpower" charges to come up with a PR campaign that would help translate my name recognition into public trust. Hard sell had come to the broker-age business; products and prices were being promoted with the same kind of zeal previously reserved for automobiles and kitchen appliances. People in the business were shocked to see an ad for Chemical Investor Services, the discount brokerage of Chemical Bank, that showed a stockbroker relaxing on his yacht as he urged a customer to buy shares. "This is the only person guaranteed to make money in the stock market," said the copy. "Whether you win or lose, he draws handsome commissions."

For advertising, the same man who had done my original ad came up with a picture of me holding a briefcase and stepping out of a cab in front of the Stock Exchange. The copy said, "Mickie's back," and referred to me as the first discount broker. Shortly after the ads started running, a letter was hand-delivered from Blaise Bozzelli, the "surveillance director" of the NYSE, ordering me to produce evidence that substantiated the accuracy of the statements in the ad, threatening to refer the matter to the "enforcement department" and demanding prior approval of any ads that ran. ("Naturally," the letter said, "there will be no fee for the prior approval review.") I would have had to pull our original floor tickets, now in deep storage, to prove that my firm had become a discount broker on May Day.

With steam coming out of my ears, I called Ace Greenberg at Bear Stearns, my clearing firm when I had gone discount, and asked him for the microfiche records verifying that I had cut commissions at the opening bell on May 1, 1975. "I remember it well," he said. "Just have the Exchange call me." I submitted a copy of the letter welcoming me to the Stock Exchange and copies of news stories from *The Wall Street Journal* and *The New York Times,* and the brouhaha went away as fast as it had started. But in my conversations with people at the Exchange, it was let slip that Leslie C. Quick, the founder of rival Quick & Reilly, had filed the complaint, on the grounds that I dealt with

---

If employees are loyal and hardworking, you want to promote from inside whenever possible.

---

institutional investors, not individuals, when I started discounting. In return, I filed a formal complaint against *his* misleading advertising, which claimed that Q&R was the "very first NYSE member firm to slash commissions." Q&R had not started discounting until June 1975—a month after me—and I challenged the "enforcers" to pursue his infraction with the same vitality and aggressiveness that was shown in coming after me. I didn't enjoy getting into such petty nonsense, but I was furious that the Big Board's sanction had cost me $15,000 in expenses for canceled ads. Ultimately, the Exchange decreed that he could say Q&R had been the first discounter "for the public," and I could say that Siebert & Co. had gone discount on the first day members of the NYSE could negotiate rates.

If employees are loyal and hardworking, you want to promote

from inside whenever possible. But the firm was in such bad shape, and I didn't know exactly who was performing well, so I needed reinforcements from outside. It's difficult to lure people from big outfits, and I often got men and women who were number two or three in their department—young "tigers" who wanted to run their own show. I had a reputation for paying the highest bonuses on the Street. People knew that if I succeeded, they would succeed with me; if I made money, I'd spread it around. The danger was in getting people who knew only how to delegate. Small-company staffers have to know how to do the job themselves. Large firms have checks and balances, and if you make a mistake, the system protects you. At a small firm, errors can be disastrous.

During my time in government, it felt as if I had turned the reins of my life over to somebody else and said, "Here, you drive for a while." That is not a customary M.O. for me, and it felt

If I made money, I'd spread it around.

good to be in charge again. I think the people at Siebert & Co. were glad to have Siebert back too, but I neither expected nor received a welcoming committee from anybody else on the Street. The big boys had usurped a lot of my territory, so I had to be innovative. If you can't play with the big boys' ball, start your own game. In November 1984 we began running ads in *The Wall Street Journal* guaranteeing prompt and courteous service, or else the next trade would be free. It wasn't claimed very often, but it had the benefit of putting my people on notice, because I wanted to know: When did the customer call? How long was he

If you can't play with the big boys' ball, start your own game.

on hold? And who held him up? In 1986 we started Siebert Quotes, making stock and option quotes available twenty-four hours a day from any push-button telephone. There was the added advantage of being able to store a client's cost per share with each stock added to the phone list, calculating the percentage gain or loss versus the current market price. That same year, we started offering one-eighth of a point commission base—the lowest commission schedule in the discount brokerage industry.

By this time, discounters were no longer looked upon as pariahs. If I had returned to a firm that hadn't been damaged or mismanaged, it would have been much bigger because the industry had grown so much in that time, and that growth had kept the firm alive. By the summer of 1985, we had fifty thousand active accounts, mostly individuals. The sweetest of those were the accounts that I bought from a rival discount brokerage started by three former officials of my firm while I was S.O.B. In 1981, in the aftermath of disputes about the treatment of long-term clients, Georgi Michele, Cathy Bennardo and William Ryff had walked out with proprietary information and client lists to start their own firm called Parr Securities. I had hired Michele back as a consultant when I returned to the firm because her memory of what had occurred was valuable. But I later learned she'd ordered that her phone not be taped—the only employee excused—when Siebert & Co. installed the new taping system to eliminate customer errors. While I was at the banking department, former clients would call to say that they were being enticed to open accounts at Parr, with insinuations that they would be better treated because I would never be returning to run my brokerage myself. I called the man managing my blind trust with every intention of suing. "I can't sue on behalf of the superintendent of banking," he said.

"Can't you sue on behalf of the firm?" I asked.

"It's inappropriate," he replied. "When you went to Banking, it was the first time that the New York Stock Exchange allowed a member firm to be put in a blind trust. If the money means that much to you, you must quit your job, go back to the firm, and *then* we can sue."

I was so angry that I considered doing just that, but ultimately I decided that the problems of the savings banks were so important that I shouldn't abandon the job. Parr quickly engendered controversy over its ads, with copy such as "We Do Floors" and "Fast Women." The NYSE received letters questioning their taste and judgment, and three years later, the SEC shut them down, amid charges of fraudulent government securities transactions and other violations. In June 1985 I bought their five hundred active accounts for $5,000. A week earlier, I had paid $100,000 for the four thousand active accounts of Bevill, Bresler & Schulman, a New Jersey brokerage that had closed shop and filed for Chapter 11 bankruptcy. Its three major partners pleaded the Fifth Amendment when the SEC brought charges of fraud and self-dealing. I got calls until midnight from friends on Wall Street who warned against the deal. I *knew* it was a risk. But I was gambling that the BBS name was not so tainted that I would be tarred. You see an opportunity and step up to the plate.

Sometimes the crooks are the clients. We deal with customers at all kinds of income levels. Some have accounts called "Funds in Advance," which means that we don't do the trade unless we have the money first—maybe because they're young and don't have a credit rating, or because they've had to declare bankruptcy or had some credit problem in the past. When the assets are built up, they may be able to buy and sell stocks relative to the funds in the account. We also use two services downtown before we open an account: We give them the prospective

---

You see an opportunity and step up to the plate.

---

client's social security number, and they run it in their computers. If that person has cheated a firm or had financial problems, chances are the computers in one of those two places will start sending out red warning flares. If that happens, we always inform the prospective customer and give him or her a chance to explain.

Over the years we have had a dozen crooks. One, a computer expert, owned a thinly traded stock (in tight supply) that he wanted to see go up in price so that he could make money. He found a way to get through the automated order system by Touch-Tone phone, entering a large order for another account. Our clerk on the Exchange floor saw the order and called to say, "We can't place that order—it would run the stock." The transaction seemed strange, so we called the client whose account number had been used. It was not his order. We took the order out and started looking around. We knew from our stock listings which customers owned that stock. And we had a sophisticated enough phone service that we could find out the origin of the call to buy, although it took a day or two. The man who was trying to run the stock happened to call that afternoon, claiming to be the client whose account number he was using and asking if we'd executed the order. When the phone records came in, we froze the account, kicked it out and reported it to the regulators.

That's all we could do; you can't sell out a client's personal position. But you can tell him he has three days to find another broker and get out. Then his name goes to those two services downtown. If this scam was attempted today with the new electronic systems, it might have gone unnoticed. But there was a human being on the floor noticing that this was not the proper-size order. Oh, you could build a computer system that stipulates the average trading volume of a stock and is rigged to sound an alarm if an order goes wildly over. But there's still a place for humans in the business.

For years after I bought a seat on the Big Board, I could not find one in a private club. The many gentlemen's clubs of New York (more than 150 at the turn of the twentieth century) had operated, unchallenged, by their own standards of pomp and privilege. As a writer in the early 1900s said, "One is likely to meet doctors, but never a dentist . . . lawyers, but not solicitors . . .

wholesale merchants, but not retail." The oldest social club in the city, the Union Club, first opened its doors—to only a privileged few—in 1836. When a member of the club killed a policeman during an argument, his friends hid him inside the building, then spirited him off to South America until the furor died down.

By the 1970s, women were sometimes permitted to enter these hallowed halls, but they were limited to certain hours or shoved into specific nooks and crannies—usually the ladies' dining room. (One woman invited to lecture at the University Club sat down in the lobby with a colleague but was asked to keep moving. Women were allowed in the lobby, but only in transit.) When I was at the banking department, the nemesis of many professional women in Albany was a graceful mansion one block from the State Capitol that was home to the men-only Fort Orange Club, where much of the local political wheeling and dealing took place.

The situation reached critical mass just after I bought the seat, when I showed up at the Union League Club on Park Avenue for a board meeting of the Sales Executives Club. I was the second female member: Joan Crawford had preceded me (on a Valentine's Day, amid many red roses) for her work on the board of Pepsi-Cola, which her husband, Alfred Steele, had run from 1955 until his death in 1959. Arriving for the meeting, I was told by the doorman that I had to go through the kitchen and walk up the back stairs: Women were not permitted in the elevators. The Union League was said to be proud of its four prohibitions: no women, no dogs, no reporters and no Democrats. I seethed through the meeting—I didn't even know what the agenda was—and some of the men asked why I was so angry. To their credit, they suggested accompanying me on the way out, but they were not permitted on the elevator with me, and in protest the group of us left by walking down the stairs and through the kitchen.

The city's human rights law already forbade discrimination in public accommodations but exempted private clubs. The criteria for this definition were rather loose. Defenders of the practice suggested that excluded groups form their own exclusive clubs rather than force their presence where they were not wanted—in other words, the myth of "separate but equal." That was no solution at all for people who knew of the advantages that accrued from business that went on behind closed doors, the very reason that companies often paid for club memberships. (An article in *Fortune* magazine once rated private clubs according to the size of the transaction that was likely to take place in the relative privacy of a club lunch between the soup and the cigar: "At the Metropolitan or the Union League or the University, you might do a $10,000 deal, but you'd use the Knickerbocker or the Union or the Racquet for $100,000, and then for $1 million you'd have to move on to the Brook or the Links.") Wives and other female relatives of Union League members were permitted to use "a delightful ladies' dining room" on the fourth floor, according to the club secretary, Kenneth Agnew. Despite the fact that women were banned from using the lockers, steam rooms, squash courts or bedrooms, Agnew announced, "We like ladies," and insisted, "We don't feel that anybody is being discriminated against in any way."

The City Council of New York disagreed, and councilwoman Carol Bellamy proposed legislation prohibiting discrimination against women and minorities at private clubs. The bill was attacked by the City Council's general welfare committee chairman, Samuel Horwitz, who said that it constituted an intrusion by the chief executive into the legislative branch of city government. He also said that it wouldn't pass, despite the fact that the bill's twenty-two sponsors appeared at the news conference called by Mayor Ed Koch to announce the bill, including such local government luminaries as Fernando Ferrer, Ruth Messinger, Sal Albanese and Noach Dear. I was invited to testify in front of the Council and reminded those present that the industry and vigor of our city was due to the efforts of Irish and

Germans and Italians, Jews and Protestants and Catholics and Moslems—*both men and women*—who came here for freedom and opportunity. "Shouldn't our clubs reflect that?" I asked.

In September 1983, Mayor Koch signed Executive Order No. 69 prohibiting the conduct of city business at private clubs that engaged in discriminatory membership practices. One year later, on October 24, 1984, he signed local law No. 63, forbidding discrimination in clubs that were not distinctly private, with simple standards based on total membership, regular meal service and income from nonmembers. (I have the pen he used.) But it wasn't until five years later, after the United States Supreme Court unanimously upheld the New York law, that the good gray Union League agreed to admit women.

And, astonishingly, it's still standing.

Three basic federal laws had governed banking in this country for half a century, named after the legislators who wrote them: The McFadden Act of 1927 bans banks and their holding companies from branching across state lines. The Glass-Steagall Act of 1933 (the same year Prohibition was repealed) forbids brokerages to accept deposits and banks to underwrite securities; it was created in the wake of the great crash to halt bank speculation in the stock market. With these New Deal restrictions, Congress erected a seemingly impenetrable wall between the securities and banking industries to punish overzealous lenders and speculators, and to prevent the excesses that had shuttered thousands of banks. In effect, one industry was divided into two.

The 1978 International Banking Act did open up a small escape clause in McFadden, permitting U.S. banks that are organized primarily to finance international operations (known as Edge Act organizations) to operate in more than one state. And by the early 1980s, several things were happening that drove a wedge into Glass-Steagall: Citibank began offering a new personal asset account called Focus, which provided discount bro-

kerage using Quick & Reilly. Charles Schwab was bought by
Bank of America (which had turned down the company's request
for a loan—twice). Security Pacific Bank of California set up a
subsidiary to do discount brokerage; Chase Manhattan announced it would buy the discount brokerage Rose and Company; and several thrift organizations got together to form Invest,
a brokerage operation that offered discounted transaction execution and investment advice. Chemical Bank began executing
stock trades for customers using a division of Donaldson, Lufkin
& Jenrette to clear transactions. Prudential Bache, one of the
largest securities firms—and an expansion of the first company
where I ever worked—proposed an alliance with commercial
banks, leasing space in bank branches and splitting commissions.

In May 1983 I managed another first by becoming the first
discount broker to set up shop in the lobby of a bank: the First
Women's Bank, in its prime midtown Manhattan location at
Fifty-seventh and Park. (Discount brokers didn't give investment
advice and thus were exempt from Glass-Steagall.) It was a perfect fit: Investors wouldn't be trading with hastily trained bank
employees, or be limited to the bank's cash investments, or have
to pay higher commissions to cover the bank's overhead. And
they were not required to open a bank account. But some clients
don't trust brokers and want to hold their own stock certificates;
this way they can buy their shares and put them right into a safe
deposit box. The bank got a percentage of our broker's commission. The first day the signs were put up, two people walked in to
place orders but had to be turned away because the applications
and order forms hadn't arrived yet.

Certainly the time had come when banks were getting into the
brokerage business, and brokers were getting into banking services. (Even outsiders were getting in on the act: Sears, Roebuck
and Company had recently bought Dean Witter Reynolds Organization, Inc. The word went out: "You can get everything from
socks to stocks.") The reaction from an officer of one New York
bank was typical: "Any bank that aids and abets the enemy by

offering a competitor's services will get what it deserves. It's letting the fox into the chicken coop." But federal regulators were unable to agree even on what a bank is. In December 1982 Dreyfus Mutual Fund, which then was worth $10 billion, bought the Lincoln State Bank in Orange, New Jersey. When the Federal Reserve Board objected, Dreyfus claimed that Lincoln was a "nonbank" because it had stopped offering certain banking services, and the FDIC approved the purchase.

The lines of demarcation among financial institutions were blurring beyond recognition, and a whole new set of rules was required. We needed regulation by function, not by institution; what we had was regulation by legal loophole. In June 1981 I went to Washington to testify before the Senate Banking Committee. I made *a lot* of suggestions: Barriers to interstate banking should be eliminated, and banks should be freed from regulations that limited their operations yet did not apply to their competitors—the mutual funds, brokerage houses, insurance companies and other financial institutions that offered the same services. Insurers were invisible bankers. The insurance industry had $1 trillion in assets but was the only financial industry untouched by antitrust statutes. I recommended changing the definition of a bank to include *any* institutions that take deposits or make commercial loans; all regulations governing one financial institution should govern all others with similar functions. "Let the Glass-Steagall Act go the way of the raccoon coat and bathtub gin," I declared (rather melodramatically, I admit). "The artifice of a nonbank bank has no place in a well-ordered financial system, and state boundaries have come to mean as much in financial terms as a wave in the ocean." But while I welcomed the blurring of lines between the banking, securities and insurance industries, I was concerned about new privacy issues. Suppose I had a heart attack listed on my insurance records—would a bank owned by the same institution make me a loan?

I proposed that the current troika of regulators overseeing the banking industry—the Federal Reserve, the Office of Thrift Supervision and the Office of the Comptroller of the Currency—be consolidated under one agency to provide better protection for consumers and allow the banks to compete with other financial institutions. Since the Fed has a built-in conflict of interest in trying to regulate the industry while setting monetary policy, all federal banking regulatory activities could be combined under the Comptroller of the Currency. The danger of concentrating too much power in one agency could be overcome with strong *state* regulatory bodies. I also recommended consolidating the insurance activities of the FDIC and the FSLIC, doing away with the Federal Home Loan Association. The various federal agencies compete with one another and with state banking regulators, so banks shop around for the agency with the most liberal policies on a specific issue. (Senator William Proxmire called it "competition in laxity.") It's certain—and entirely proper—that an aggressive banking executive will seek and find the weakest link in the regulatory chain to accomplish the bank's business objectives. But that's no way to protect consumers or the safety of the system.

Sympathy for the banks was scarce in Washington. The industry had sponsored a ham-handed campaign to repeal the withholding of taxes on interest and dividends, a move that had incurred the wrath of the Reagan Administration. Congress was angry that bad loans to developing nations were forcing government to bail out the banks with resources from the International Monetary Fund. Banks paid taxes of an average 2.6 percent on their income, compared to 44 percent for the auto industry. Their behavior elicited public sympathy commonly reserved for landlords and umpires.

Small banks were opposed to interstate banking because they feared being swallowed up by the giants—Citibank, for instance, had recently announced the purchase of a small bank in South Dakota. And the chairman of the Senate Banking Committee, Senator Jake Garn, was opposed to interstate banking to protect his Utah banking constituents, who might have looked pretty yummy to the same kind of big bad wolves that had moved on South Dakota. Garn had no objection to letting banks and securities firms compete in each other's territories, provided the change was properly structured. But he argued that the country was not ready for such financial fraternization and that there would be no more than ten or twelve congressmen willing to vote for the repeal of the McFadden Act permitting interstate banking.

Treasury Secretary Donald Regan favored a gradual approach toward ending cross-state and cross-country prohibitions, beginning in such natural markets as New York, Connecticut and New Jersey. He proposed letting banks expand into other activities of a financial nature—as determined by the Federal Reserve—by setting up subsidiaries of a bank holding company to cover insurance underwriting and brokerage, real estate investment and development, and securities functions. Small banks (with less than $100 million in assets) would be allowed to perform securities activities through direct subsidiaries without having to set up holding companies.

Five years later the Federal Reserve Board allowed banks with brokerage subsidiaries to provide investment advice to retail customers, further blurring the line between broker and banker. Dire forecasts were made about the discount brokerage business in the wake of these changes, much as the Cassandras had lamented the advent of discounting. Some predicted that banks would take over discount brokerage, in pursuit of lucrative fee income and new customers. Sure, it meant more competition, but it also created more customers. Banks would be offering advice to clients who'd never invested before.

There were other changes in the business that I found far more ominous. In the mid-1980s, Wall Street was dominated by people like Ivan Boesky, Michael Milken and other corporate raiders, whose leviathan deals were having a negative effect on the small investor. Boesky's bailiwick was risk arbitrage: purchasing shares of companies involved or rumored to be prospects in upcoming mergers, takeover bids, leveraged buyouts or liquidations, with the expectation of selling the shares at a higher price when one of those transactions was consummated. The rash of corporate takeover moves benefited only big business. Individuals were investing in stocks that appreciated in value but then plummeted after the raiders moved in, and management bought them out to keep the peace.

Milken was the "junk bond king." He developed a way to finance riskier companies, and some major companies got their start that way. But he and his partners got greedy. When they did a deal, they often created a partnership that bought bonds for itself and held them, telling customers that those bonds were oversold and kicking them out at a profit a few days later. In June 1985, I testified (again) before the Senate Banking Committee that junk bonds should carry a warning label reading "Hazardous to your financial health." Fred Joseph, the chief executive of Drexel Burnham Lambert, which made the market in junk bonds, sent me a letter saying I didn't know what I was talking about. Well, Drexel's not around anymore, and neither is Joseph: The brokerage pleaded guilty to six counts of fraud and paid $650 million in fines and penalties. Joseph himself was banned from running a securities firm following Drexel's collapse. By 1986 Boesky was secretly taping conversations with other arbitragers and junk-bond dealers for the SEC in exchange for leniency in his insider trading scandal; he ended up paying $100 million as part of a negotiated settlement but didn't escape prison time. In 1990 Milken was escorted out of the Drexel building at 55 Broad Street by SEC officers and convicted of fraud and racketeering. Some of the companies he financed became quite successful, and some went broke. He was really a genius at finding a void and filling it, but as often happens, greed became the creed.

Congress had ordered the government to sell its 85 percent interest in Conrail (Consolidated Rail Corporation), which had a virtual monopoly on train service in the Northeast and Midwest. The company had been created in 1976 from the remnants of Penn Central Transportation Company and six other failing and bankrupt railroad systems in the northeastern corridor. In 1981 the Reagan Administration was planning a national yard sale of up to $40 billion in government loans and billions more in property, from oil fields to radio frequencies, and it was looking to Conrail as a linchpin in its privatization program. Congress saw the sale as an opportunity for budget savings; Wall Street saw great financial opportunity; and the Department of Transportation, under Elizabeth Dole, wanted Conrail out of its way, since it was generally conceded that the government should not be running companies in competition with privately owned ones. In January 1987 Goldman Sachs was chosen to administer and coordinate the sale with five comanagers: First Boston, Merrill Lynch, Morgan Stanley, Salomon Brothers and Shearson Lehman. Under an amendment to the Conrail Privatization Act, the Department of Transportation was required to name six minority-owned financial-services firms to a special underwriting bracket, each partnered with one of the lead managers. That was an unheard-of arrangement on Wall Street. These six would share some of the duties and divide 10 percent of the management fees, which were expected to total approximately $70 million. But women were not considered a minority.

It was the first time in almost twenty years that I said, "I'm a woman. Deal me in." I went to Dole and said it was totally unfair that no woman-owned business was to be included. I was told that when the senior underwriters filed, I should call and ask for the documents that would be given to any of the firms applying for the special bracket position. I got the forms, filled them out and made a presentation to Goldman Sachs. I knew my firm was more qualified than many of the applicants for the minority slots: I had gotten started and was able to buy a seat because I knew equities. I had retail accounts and could give the Conrail stock the wide distribution that the government wanted.

Most of the minority firms started in the bond business. It was a good argument, and Siebert & Co. was accepted as the only woman-owned firm; the other five in the special bracket were owned by blacks or Hispanics.

After getting a "due diligence" report the size of the Manhattan phone book, I obtained a $5 million secured loan from Chemical Bank to handle the deal and signed papers pledging everything I owned, including my apartment. We were warned not to make any public statements about the IPO until Goldman Sachs gave the go-ahead that the "red herring" prospectus had been filed with the SEC. (It featured a lovely color photo of a Conrail train against a background of fall foliage, rounding the scenic Horseshoe Curve near Altoona, Pennsylvania.) Until that filing was declared effective, we could make only oral offers to potential buyers.

Perhaps it was an inauspicious sign that the red herring was dated February 13, 1987—Friday the thirteenth. Each of the six coleads agreed to a buddy system with one of the minority firms and to conduct the offering so that the special bracket had an opportunity to participate to a *significant* (their word, not mine) degree. I was assigned to First Boston. The big brothers were supposed to share their research and technical advice, and assist the minority firms in carrying out their duties and achieving their goals. But we felt that the selling process was not being managed in a manner consistent with the intentions of the Privatization Act. For starters, each of the special brackets was permitted to send a rep to only one of the series of private meetings with potential institutional investors, known as "the road show." We were originally limited to 200,000 shares each, despite language in the act that guaranteed each firm a retention fully commensurate with its sales capabilities. Including the loan, I had enough assets to carry the entire obligation and knew I could place that amount plus more.

Some of the majority firms had promised loans to the minority firms. But just before the plan was approved, they retracted their offers, saying it might constitute a conflict of interest. The special-bracket group agreed to lower the bar and underwrite only 50,000 shares each. But then one of the firms didn't have even that much capital, and then another, Daniels & Bell, wanted to go back to the original 200,000. I said I would do that too. I did offer a capital infusion of $125,000 to the Hispanic firm AIBC Financial Corp., whose president, José Antonio Alvarado, was an incredibly bright Harvard-educated economics professor from Nicaragua, where he'd been ambassador to the Vatican at the tender age of twenty-one and ambassador to the United Nations four years later. I felt simpatica, as though we were both on the outside looking in. But my offer was frowned on by the managing underwriters. We drew up a mailing list of minority organizations that might wish to participate in the offering and did our own mini–road shows, some in Spanish, but it was all fairly ineffective. Since several of the black-owned firms dealt exclusively in bonds, they didn't know the institutions that bought stock. I knew which major financial institutions wanted to buy the stock on the offering and told the minority firms whom to call on the equity trading desks. (The senior partner of one of the underwriting firms called and asked if I was getting a kickback. I told him he was talking to the former New York superintendent of banking and slammed down the phone.) Outreach to potential female investors was even more difficult because so few of them owned businesses, and none of them had available the kind of funds needed to come to this party. I wrote to Harrison J. Goldin, controller of New York City, since it was likely that various pension plans of the city would purchase Conrail stock in the IPO, and I wanted to get some of the orders. I sent a blind carbon copy to Mayor Ed Koch, since Goldin had previously told me he did not influence who did business with the city pension funds, but nothing came of it.

In the end, I placed all of the stock and made some money— the first major underwriting in which my firm participated.

Donald R. Gant, the president of Goldman Sachs, sent me a memento of the deal: a Lucite block enclosing a copy of the cover page of the prospectus. I was playing with the big boys, but I was angry that I'd had to fight to get into the underwriting. When the sale was completed in March 1987, private investors ended up paying $1.65 billion for the largest stock offering in Wall Street history: 52 million shares in the United States and more than 6 million in other countries. A congressional aide who played a key role in shaping the legislation governing the deal said, "Before this, I think there was a mystical belief that New York bankers are brighter than most others. Instead they are a bunch of shlocks, with fewer principles—and greedier to boot." But that remark was too flip. Conrail was a particularly sensitive transaction, and there were a lot of honorable people trying to do it justice. Also a few piggies.

In 1987 the United States Supreme Court ruled that federally chartered banks could expand their discount brokerage businesses by opening securities offices nationwide, legalizing something the banks had been doing all along. Of course, anything that happened in 1987 was moot after Black Monday, October 19.

8

STAND BY TO CRASH

*If the client goes under,
you're the senior partner.*

When I went to the banking department, I agreed to "ABC" my Stock Exchange seat, signing a contract with a floor broker to use the membership while I was away. Under the terms of the agreement, this man had the right to buy the seat. The contract was a mistake—it could have been the error of the accountant or the consultant I was working with at the time. But when I came back to the firm, I didn't know enough to have it changed. The buyer exercised his right early in 1987, waited until he had a guaranteed profit, then "flipped" the seat, reselling it the same day. Emotionally, it was a big deal: At one point, being a member had meant a lot to me. But professionally, it wasn't that significant. The rules had changed since I had joined the Exchange. Any firm could lease a seat or qualify by affiliating with an independent broker, and electronic members were permitted, with all the rights and obligations of memberships but no floor member.

By 1987 Siebert & Co. had good capital, and we were getting ready to expand, open some branches. I never took much money out of the business. The firm was a Subchapter S. That's basically a designation that allows a small company to have the benefits of a corporation in limiting liability—only the firm, not an individual, is liable in the event of a judgment—but you must pay taxes as an individual. The tax bite could be higher or lower than it would be for a corporation. I had enough money. My investments provided a nice standard of living that I could easily afford, so I let most of my money accumulate in the firm. I didn't owe a dime personally; I didn't even have a mortgage. Having learned my lesson in 1962, when I was hardly more than a trainee and saw $500,000 of stocks bought on margin go down the tubes, I vowed never to owe that kind of money again. I had put my money in three piles: quality stocks that I owned outright, stocks that were margined and convertible bonds carried at a 10 percent margin (then allowed). When I went to Banking, I had reduced the margin because I couldn't concentrate on the market, and, besides, I'm not a trader. I said I would never touch stocks I owned outright to meet a margin call, and I had lived that way. I was bringing in accounts, the firm was expanding, and I let the capital grow.

The Dow Jones reached an all-time high of 2,722 points on August 25, 1987. The Big Board was handling a huge, unexpected volume of trading that summer, up to 600 million shares a day. But on Monday, October 19, the Dow dropped 508 points, crashing to 1,738—the largest drop in one day ever, exceeding even the one immediately preceding the Great Depression. The financial markets lost $636 billion that day—to be known forever as Black Monday—and the figure was $1.173 trillion since the August 25 high. John J. Phelan, Jr., chairman of the NYSE, called it "the nearest thing to a meltdown I ever want to see." I was watching the waves of selling on the ticker. My office was on the second floor of the *Newsweek* building on Madison Avenue, and the thing that kept me sane was looking out the window at the people on the street acting as if the world had *not* ended: buying hot dogs from the corner vendor, strolling out of boutiques with shopping bags, catching the uptown bus. Life was going on.

Finger-pointing and recriminations about the day's volatility focused on two technical instruments: program trading and portfolio insurance, both financial techniques that use complicated high-tech/high-stakes strategies affecting innumerable stocks. Program trading, authorized in 1982, is a term for the use of computers to make simultaneous quick trades of large blocks of stock and can involve large amounts of index futures and options. It's essentially arbitrage: The market's highest rollers, usually big-money brokerage houses and professional traders, take advantage of price differences between securities traded in New York and corresponding stock index futures traded on the Chicago Mercantile Exchange, where the most widely used futures products are traded. Contracts are bought and sold according to someone's belief in which way the actual stock market will move on a set date. Futures prices often move more dramatically than stock prices as traders try to anticipate market swings. Now it's become a completely automated process, with computers in brokerage houses programmed to buy or sell the instant a designated price gap is detected between stocks and futures. Program traders have no interest in stock prices; they only want to narrow the discrepancy between two prices for the same basket of stocks. Some people, like former Fed chairman Paul Volcker, not to mention lots of individual investors, thought that their buying and selling practices had precipitated the roller-coaster ride of Black Monday.

Others said: Not so fast. In a report on the market turmoil, the Commodity Futures Trading Commission (arguably a biased source) said that only about 9 percent of the stocks sold on October 19 were associated with index arbitrage and suggested that the larger villain was portfolio insurance. This was the brainstorm of Hayne Leland, a young finance professor at the University of California at Berkeley, who was obsessed about his family's financial vulnerability. It was supposed to be a way of "hedging" and minimizing investment loss, with clients paying something akin to an insurance premium. Beginning with Leland's company in 1980—and followed by a host of imitators—an investor was automatically shifted out of a position when it began to fall, selling a certain number of stock index futures in stages determined by computer and "insuring" the client against losing more than a predetermined amount.

Portfolio insurance worked in theory, but when put to the test in the real world, with huge unanticipated volume, it overwhelmed the market as it was dropping and compounded the damage of October 19. Many managers of "insured" portfolios thought they were protected from a market decline, but when futures prices collapsed right from the opening bell, some panicked and started dumping stocks at whatever price could be had. One large company sold a dozen baskets of $100 million each.

Many of the largest investors in the stock market—the pension funds, once considered overfunded because of huge stock gains—had to sit tight, perhaps with too little cash to meet their obligations. Meanwhile, small individual investors were confused about whether to buy or sell. Stock price information was running too far behind activity to be reliable, so at Siebert we accepted orders only from those willing to deal at the market price. But bids and offers were extremely thin. A large number of investors moved their stock-based investments into mutual funds, primarily money markets that invested in short-term fixed-income instruments such as government securities and CDs. As Gertrude Stein said, "Money is always there, but the pockets change."

On Tuesday, October 20, the Dow rebounded by 102 points. Stocks regained $60 billion of the previous day's free fall, but the stock price of nearly every major brokerage house tumbled. The big companies began a weeklong trend of buying back their own stock at bargain prices. On Wednesday, October 21, the Dow soared a record 186 points, and the market regained half the

---

"Money is always there, but the pockets change."

---

ground it had lost in Monday's plunge. But on Thursday, October 22, the market dropped again, and the Dow closed 77 points down in heavy trading. Responding to the wild fluctuations and avalanche of trading activity—and largely to catch up with the crush of paperwork—the NYSE and the American Stock Exchange announced shorter hours for three days, ending at 2:00 P.M. rather than at 4:00 P.M. "The system needs time to catch its breath," said Phelan, and the move was endorsed by the SEC. Ronald Reagan declared that the frenetic activity was "purely a stock market thing."

On Friday, October 23, the Dow weakly managed to close less than one point up, but there was a pervasive mood of "Thank God It's Friday." The shorter hours and limits on selling helped restore relative calm. TV crews were camped outside the NYSE at two o'clock waiting for people to pour out in droves, but they didn't. "What do they think?" one trader was heard to say. "The bell rings and it's recess? Trading stopped; work didn't." That week, a record 2.3 billion shares had changed hands, and in brokerages all over the city, people came to work on Saturday just to help with the paperwork backlog. But *The New York Times* was referring to the feeling of a "plague city" with panicked denizens and overcompensatory behavior—full bars and bad jokes. (What's the difference between October 28, 1929, and October 19, 1987? Answer: In 1987, it's the computers that are jumping out the window. What's the difference between a yuppie and pigeon? Answer: A pigeon can still make a deposit on a BMW.)

One of the Rothschilds is credited with saying that the time to buy is when there's blood in the streets or when the cannons are at the gates of Paris. Two days after the crash, I went into the office and announced, "Let's buy stocks!" I didn't owe any money personally, nor did my firm. But we were in trouble. There were clients whose accounts were underwater because of the margin, and we were responsible if they couldn't pay. Nobody had imagined a drop of such magnitude so fast or anticipated a "short squeeze": investors who decide to act on a stock take either a short or long position. A long position implies a belief (and hope) that the price will rise. But short sellers borrow shares that they believe are overpriced and will go down, selling what they do not own with the understanding (or hope) that they'll be able to buy them back at a lower price. The firm they're doing business with must borrow the shares, whether from other clients or another firm, and the short seller pays interest on the value of the shares. SEC rules allow investors to sell short only on an "uptick" (when the last trade is higher than the preceding one for a security) or a "zero-plus tick" (when the price is the same as the previous one, which had to be a plus tick). If the stock starts shooting up, the shorts try to buy back as soon as possible to stem their losses. If they can't cover their obligations, they can be wiped out in one day. Under the rules of the SEC, if an account goes under and has a negative balance, the firm is responsible for the losses. In effect, it is the lender of last resort.

I was clearing through a subsidiary of Security Pacific Bank called FICS, which was required to report the problem to the NYSE (the clearinghouse is financially responsible to my firm and to the customers). A meeting was set up with several small firms that were in trouble, each of us in separate rooms at the Stock Exchange. Most of our dilemma came from one account for a man I shall call Smith-Jones, who had a large margin. A couple of weeks before, he'd hit three or four other firms, buying blocks of stocks. Two weeks before, he'd had plenty of excess cash in his Siebert account. A week or two before the crash, he'd been able to draw out around $400,000 that had never gotten recorded. It had gone into a "suspense" account, where money is put if the margin clerk or cashiering department doesn't know what account to credit or debit—or basically doesn't know whose account it is.

A few days later, Smith-Jones called to ask, "What's my margin?" and was told that he had an excess. He took out a similar amount, but the clearing firm found the "error" early in the week, adjusted the account—which was now short—and issued a margin call. He brought in 219,000 shares of a low-priced NASDAQ-listed stock to meet the margin call, and FICS double-booked it as *two times* 219,000 shares. That happened the Monday before the market break. His account looked as though it was in great shape, but when the error was discovered and the market broke, the account was left with a balance of zero *minus* several million dollars, for which I was responsible.

A fiat came from the Stock Exchange: We had to settle with our clearing firm, or we would not be allowed to open for business the next day. I wanted to fight. I felt it was more than a coincidence that the same kind of error had happened twice in the same account. I believed that there had to be some serious cooperation between the customer and the FICS back office. I thought Smith-Jones might have paid off the margin clerk. (FICS later went out of business. Incompetent or crooked? I'll never know.) For a large brokerage, the Exchange had to overlook this kind of problem. One of the big boys couldn't be closed up overnight, and it could limp along with reduced or no capital. My firm would not be granted such a reprieve, nor would any other small firm, and the NYSE was not about to cut me any slack for being its first woman. In fact, I was told that if I had to close my doors, the Exchange was perfectly capable of handling the press. I was given overnight to decide what to do.

I called my lawyer, Bill Shea, the senior partner and founder of Shea Gould and the namesake for Shea Stadium. "I'm in trouble," I said, and he canceled all his other appointments that day to go over the facts with me.

"How much money are you worth outside the firm?" he asked. I told him. "You don't have enough money to fight Security Pacific," he said. "The bank's lawyers will have you in court until you're bone dry. You have a good business. Settle, roll up your sleeves, and make the money back." He never charged me one penny for his time, and better advice I've never had. But the settlement really cleaned my firm out, taking all the capital except $1 million, which was more than what I needed as a firm clearing on a fully disclosed basis. And it stopped our expansion. You're not the client's partner if he's making money, but if he goes under, you are the senior partner.

There were worse casualties because of Smith-Jones: His partner had an account with a discount firm that cleared through L. F. Rothschild & Co. and had major margin calls. I'm told it broke the discounter, and the fine old firm of Rothschild

---

You're not the client's partner if he's making money, but if he goes under, you are the senior partner.

---

went out of business shortly thereafter. As for Smith-Jones, I called him at home on a Saturday after the dust settled. "I know what you did," I told him, "and if I knew anyone to do it, I'd send him over to break your kneecaps." I *didn't* know anyone, but if I had, Mr. Smith-Jones might have been limping for a while.

We had other clients who came in crying, lying and begging, swearing they'd said "Sell," not "Buy," but all our phone calls were recorded, so we could back up our position. One client who owed thousands skipped town for Florida, and I had to hire a collection agency to find him. Another client in Louisiana started Black Monday with $200,000 and ended up $400,000 in the hole. He sued us for gross negligence, claiming he could not get through on the phone to liquidate his position. But the judge ruled that he had to make up the deficit, agreeing with me that he was not the only genius in the United States of America who knew the secret of snatching victory from the jaws of defeat that day. She said that accepting the "busy signal" defense would open a floodgate that would make it impossible for any securities broker to collect a debit balance.

After writing off $2 million in bad debts to bail out the accounts, paying legal and other huge expenses, we still made $273,000 in 1987. Other firms did much worse: By the end of October, E. F. Hutton was publicly denying a rumor that it had lost $100 million in government bond trading and faced bankruptcy. The chief financial officer of the company said that it had lost about $20 million since the first of the month, prompting an employee to remark, "Great, that means we've only lost a little more than $1 million a day." In the three months between Labor Day and Thanksgiving, more than half a trillion dollars (that's trillion with a *t*) in stock prices was wiped out. I had never seen a market slide so fast, and even though it rebounded, the retail part of our business went down by 50 percent, as the little guy went on vacation from the market.

It was not a nice experience, but it held me in very good stead. I felt that, at best, our clearing firm had not been on top of the margin and vowed that in the future we would not depend on any firm to manage the risk; we would, in effect, do our own margin calculations, since our capital was on the line. In any game where there are winners, there have to be losers, and it's no disgrace to lose. But you're not entitled to make the same mistake twice. Today we run the business differently: We had software made to help us see any risks in the accounts more easily. We know every day— *during* the day, in real time—where the markets are and what our clients' positions are. Sometimes we can warn them before our clearing house warns us because we are so sensitive to that kind of information. Timing is critical. If you own stocks outright, you're

---

In any game where there are winners, there
have to be losers, and it's no disgrace to lose.
But you're not entitled to make the
same mistake twice.

---

not disadvantaged if the market drops. Yes, you lose money on paper. But if you're on borrowed money and don't have assets to back it up, if you have to sell to reduce your margin, you could be selling at the bottom. I never allowed myself to borrow large amounts of money again, and I am less aggressive in the market. I emerged a little shell-shocked and wanting a better reserve. And I'll always have some bonds. There's nothing like having a good stream of income that pays all your living expenses.

Big Board Chairman Phelan had compared the market to a patient who is having chest pains and is told to make changes in his diet and exercise so he doesn't have a heart attack. I knew there ought to be more limitations on computerized trading. Options and futures add nothing to the economy of the United States. They allow corporations in certain circumstances to hedge their costs, but they do not in themselves foster growth, and they do not create jobs, except for brokers. A Texas newspaper editorial called them "new gimcracks and gewgaws." There had been no restrictions on the number of options and futures contracts people could write, except for the size of the account and maintenance of margin, and the system became a gambling casino. Even if these instruments were not exclusively responsible for triggering and accelerating Black Monday's 508-point plunge in equity prices, they were causing swings in the market before the crash that really distorted the basic value of stocks. People who were investment-oriented started to realize that something was wrong. Ordinarily, you research a stock. You buy it on value. The earnings reports come out. They look good. You start to feel confident. The stock is up a couple of points. Then the contracts hit, and the stock is down 10 percent, off three points—for no apparent reason. The markets are much larger and more liquid today, but it doesn't take a terrorist attack by Osama bin Laden to have a devastating effect. All that's needed is several people selling a couple of hundred millions worth of futures. When that kind of thing can influence this country's ability to raise capital, something is wrong.

Individual investors were saying that they felt cheated by institutional sharpies who skimmed profits by means of sophisticated computer programs, especially those that capitalized on fleeting price gaps between shares traded in New York and stock index futures traded in Chicago. An ever-increasing percentage of the Big Board orders placed by individual shareholders are executed by the same electronic delivery system, Direct Order

Turnaround (DOT), which was originally intended to take care of the small orders. It enabled the discounters to cut rates because it was basically automated and there was no floor brokerage cost to do a trade. But on Black Monday, the institutional traders were flooding DOT with large orders. Individual customers were really screwed, waiting several hours to get an order execution back because of the volume. There was an imbalance between buy and sell orders. Now the NYSE has a rule that provides for a "matching" process called "sidecar," which involves holding or shifting orders so that there's a balance between buyers and sellers, keeping the market more stable. And orders from small investors get executed first. Institutional investors have more ways to execute an order than an individual, especially one at a computer who might not even be able to get an order through.

I found it ironic that the biggest fans of stock-index arbitrage were the institutional funds, because they'd always been slow to take a position. No quick trades for them. They had the reputation of being the most cautious, conservative people on Wall Street. But the pressure to perform on a per quarter basis just as in business was not healthy for Wall Street. From a money manager's point of view, program trading was an attractive idea. Whether you hold one hundred thousand or one million shares of stock, selling at even a fraction of a point higher can mean making a profit. The institutional investors used to bring a certain stability to the market. When they started to trade actively, volatility became the norm.

I favored having the SEC control every financial instrument that involves stocks, a recommendation made by Nicolas Brady, the treasury secretary under George Bush and head of a presidential task force assigned to investigate the crash. At the time, futures trading was overseen by the Commodity Futures Trading Commission, and its rules were less restrictive than the rules for stocks. Now you can't buy futures on margin, and if you sell a "put" (a contract describing the right to sell a specific amount at a specific price and time), you must have enough margin to cover the likelihood that the put will be exercised and the assets in your account will cover the securities coming in. At the time of the crash, and today still, a trader in index futures had to put up much less cash for a purchase than an investor buying the underlying stocks. The higher leverage made it easier to speculate, but the very purpose of capital markets—raising seed money for new ventures and supplying capital for the growth of these companies—was in jeopardy. The pool of investors to provide cash for start-up companies dried up for a while after the painful ride of '87.

The NYSE responded by directing member firms not to use the DOT system for program trading anytime the Dow moved more than fifty points in a day. In November, the market resumed unrestricted program trading, but in a January 1988 memo expressing concern about "intra-day market volatility and its impact on investor confidence," the NYSE eased off a little. It requested that all member firms refrain from using the DOT for program trading if the Dow moved seventy-five points up or down. I thought that the confidence of individual investors would be restored if institutions were not allowed to use the system *at all* for their own accounts, and I wrote to NYSE chairman Phelan, expressing my opinion that the recent restrictions did not go far enough and that program trading should be used only for small orders from public customers. I sent copies to everyone who had an account with my firm, as well as to SEC Chairman David Ruder and Fed Chairman Alan Greenspan. Some of my customers followed my lead and sent their own letters. "You either are pregnant or not," wrote one. "Program trading is either right or wrong. I think it is wrong and should be abolished." That spring, under fire from regulators and enraged investors, four major brokerages—Salomon Brothers, Paine Webber, Bear Stearns and Kidder, Peabody—all scrapped index arbitrage program trading on their own accounts. In July 1988, the NYSE and the Chicago Mercantile Exchange installed "circuit breakers": a series of automatic trading delays and halts that would take effect whenever the Dow fell a hundred points or more in one day. This measure was intended to slow down the market during a crisis and provide investors large and small with time to evaluate their trading decisions.

A big part of the Black Monday massacre for individual investors was the inaccessibility of market-makers to the NASD, the National Association of Securities Dealers. These are brokers who specialize in buying or selling particular stocks for their inventory, at that time taking most orders from retail brokers by phone. In the frenzy of the '87 crash, many market-makers simply left their phones off the hook, and the failure to communicate meant that plenty of individual investors were unable to sell their positions or to pick up beaten-down shares at suddenly attractive prices. (Several times, when my firm tried to reach a market-maker, as soon as he heard "Sell" he would slam down the phone.) All stocks listed with NASDAQ, the trading arm of the NASD that regulates over-the-counter trading, have at least three market-makers; major stocks have dozens.

In June 1988, NASD changed its rules so that multiple market-makers could post competing bids to buy and sell stocks, making it easier for brokers to find market-makers for stocks. The new rules stipulated that all firms making markets in the three thousand NASDAQ National Market System stocks must use its electronic Small Order Execution System (SOES) for appropriate orders. (Until then, using the system had been up to the broker.) Each market-maker now had to promise to buy or

---

Customers must know it might be impossible to sell in a market crisis.

---

sell on demand a minimum number of shares. Any market-maker who logged off SOES (except for a few excusable reasons, such as profuse bleeding) would be suspended for twenty trading days. (In the chaos of the 1987 crash, many simply logged off the computer, stranding their helpless investors.) It was the first step in ensuring that small investors got a fair shot in over-the-counter trading. But some Wall Streeters felt that this and other reforms were hiding the true level of risk in investing, claiming that customers must know it might be impossible to sell in a market crisis. One broker was quoted as saying, "They should be told, 'We might have to come after your Porsche or summer house.'"

9

BILLIONAIRE FOR A DAY

If you're not willing to accept the worst that can happen, don't do it.

A few years ago, the State Department asked me to visit Hungary along with several other female entrepreneurs and talk to the women of that country about running and growing a business. I told them: Write down the best that could happen and the worst that could happen; if you aren't willing to accept the worst, don't do it.

There are three four-letter words ending in *k* that are responsible for my success. One is *work*—that's obvious. The second is *luck:* When I was a trainee, I had the good fortune to be assigned to some industries that nobody else wanted, but they proved to be lucrative. The third word is *risk:* the ability to study the information, assess liability and be brave enough to make a decision. Recognizing a capacity for calculated risk is a key to success. To me, that means analyzing a situation and asking tough questions: What are the pros and cons? What do I bring to this? What are my weaknesses?

Equally important is recognizing whether a business is capable of growth. A lot of people own vibrant small companies that are a source of pride, but many of them will never be empires, and possibly with good reason. Small-business owners have to get a handle on their emotions. I've watched people use up their resources because they wouldn't face the fact that growing bigger wasn't a good idea, or that maybe they had a niche company that didn't lend itself to growth. To get big, you've got to delegate. So if you want to have your hand in everything, you've got to stick with a tiny firm. If you're going to be hands-on about anything, it should be your expenses. When I started my company, nobody got our monthly bank statement to balance until I went through every check. That way I could see what categories the expenditures fell into and could say, "Gee, our phone bills

---

To get big, you've got to delegate. So if you want to have your hand in everything, you've got to stick with a tiny firm. If you're going to be hands-on about anything, it should be your expenses.

---

are high—maybe we should use another carrier." I'm always thinking of ways to save. Certainly I've forged relationships with suppliers over the years, but no relationship is sacred. Suppliers can start to take a customer for granted.

A business owner must reappraise on a continual basis. I don't care if you're selling stocks or stockings. If sales are down and your net is down, you have to ask: What's going on here? Is it the industry? Is it the economy? Or have I made a mistake?

Suppliers can start to take a customer for granted.

Don't let emotions cloud your judgment here, either. And when things are going well, you have to reappraise and prepare for growth by training people to whom you *can* delegate. You might have a succession plan for your accountant because after you've grown you'll want someone with more sophistication.

In spring 1993, I responded to a blind ad in *The Wall Street Journal* that expressed an interest in acquiring or becoming partner in a company. It mentioned the candidate's experience in marketing, administration and operations. That's the Triple

Crown of management—it's difficult to find someone with know-how in all three areas. The ad was placed by David S. Grayson, who worked at ABN AMRO Bank, a global banking group. I'd actually met him in the mid-1980s, when I had considered selling my firm and running for the Senate again. I'd talked

---

A business owner must reappraise on a continual basis. I don't care if you're selling stocks or stockings.

---

with the chairman of the New York State Republican Party and said that if I could get the nomination without a primary, I was prepared to put up $1 million. But I was told that there were other candidates with bigger war chests—Rudolph Giuliani, Ronald Lauder—and besides, the party still didn't cotton to my position on reproductive freedom without restrictions. By the time I met with Grayson again, my firm was not for sale—we were making too much money, and I had no desire to run for public office again. But he said that he'd been a founder of Norstar Brokerage, which had started as Discount Brokerage Corporation and been bought by Norstar Bank; he'd been responsible for opening all the Norstar branches. I thought he could be invaluable in helping me establish an office in Boca Raton, Florida, by September, in time to open accounts for the affluent "snow birds" who winter in warmth. Many of them were retired New Yorkers and New Jerseyans who were familiar with my firm but had stopped doing business with us because we didn't have a Florida branch. I agreed to make Grayson president and CEO of my retail discount division and announced his position in a "tombstone ad" in the financial pages. I had just signed a lease for offices on the seventeenth floor of the unique red granite "Lipstick Building" in midtown Manhattan, doubling our space to about eight thousand square feet. We reconfigured Grayson's office to give him a window and the size of room to which he thought he was entitled.

The professional alliance was rocky from the beginning. A week before Grayson started, a weekly industry newssheet published an article saying that I was *selling* my firm to Grayson and a small brokerage called Krieger and Co. Other serious misrepresentations in the piece included an assertion that we would open fourteen or fifteen branches in major cities within two years and become the largest of the deep-discount brokerages. I asked Grayson whether or not he had spoken to *Securities Week,* and he said no. It turned out that he had, in fact, spoken with a reporter at *Wall Street Letter,* a similar kind of industry newsletter. I felt he had dissembled in not revealing that. When I asked how he could claim that we would be the biggest, he said we could create the image through television ads.

There were other things: Grayson had disconnected the taping machine on his phone that everyone else in the office had. And I learned that he was negotiating for office space on the thirty-first floor of our building, where the Krieger group was to be located. So he did have an intention to buy that firm—an arrangement that, had it gone through, would have made it impossible for him to be a hands-on manager, as he said he was. He had, in fact, written a proposal to acquire Krieger without my authorization.

Most important, it turned out that Grayson knew marketing but did not know risk management and did not seem interested in costs. Every time I'd get into a conversation with him, he'd say arrogantly, "*I'm* the president, and I don't need your approval." This was extremely untrue. His contract specifically stated: "In the performance of your responsibilities, you shall at all times be subject to the control and direction of Muriel F. Siebert, and you will consult with her in advance of making any major personnel or economic decision." Unbeknownst to me, shortly after signing this contract, he entered into a consulting agreement with another firm, one that had enough problems to keep someone busy for a long time.

About ten weeks after he started, I came into the office late one Wednesday morning to learn that Grayson was saying I'd lied to him and had broken our agreement. Unless I turned control of the company over to him that day, he was going to sue the firm and me personally for tens of millions of dollars. I tried to remain calm because I know that when someone is threatening to sue you, the best thing to do is keep your mouth shut. But when he left my office, I called my lawyer. That night as I was getting dressed to go out, my chief financial officer called to tell me that Grayson had resigned. I was shocked and said that when I got to the office the next day, we'd talk about picking up the pieces and figuring out who'd be taking on his responsibilities. But the next day Grayson claimed that he *hadn't* quit; on the contrary, he was planning to be there every day. It was crazy, but he seemed to expect that he would continue to come to the office, do some paperwork and get paid, all the while pursuing damages against me.

The matter went to arbitration at the New York Stock Exchange, with Grayson suing for $53 million. He claimed breach of contract, breach of an oral agreement to sell him 50 percent of the company's stock, damage to his career and reputation, loss of his previous position and punitive damages. All of the claims were ultimately dropped except for the breach of the employment agreement. But what infuriated me was the NYSE permitting him to pierce the corporate veil by allowing his claim against my personal assets as well as those of the company. If there had been a ruling in his favor, I would have been wiped out. I asked the NYSE to see any example of this happening to another member of the Stock Exchange in the past and was told, "You'll just have to trust us."

The night before arbitration was to begin, a good deal of information became clear: Grayson had been only a nonpaid *trainee* at Discount Broker Corporation. He falsely claimed that I had taken him away from a job that was paying him a quarter of a million dollars a year. In fact, his salary at ABN AMRO was $150,000. He was still collecting money from that firm, having never filed the U-5 form that is required when a registered rep leaves a firm or the U-4 form for beginning work at Siebert & Co.

There were sixteen full sessions of the arbitration panel, which ultimately awarded Grayson $57,115.69—almost half the amount that *I* felt he was owed as balance of what he would have earned on his one-year contract with me. And it was recommended that he be sent up for enforcement by the Exchange because of his misstatements on forms for the new partnership he established and the fact that he had never filed his registration with our firm. I went back to the NYSE and asked to see evidence that it had allowed a similar action against any man who was a member, but I received nothing. I even applied for reimbursement of my $378,874.66 in legal fees, a request that is often granted, but was denied. I am still mad about every bit of it, including the sixty-six cents.

As of 1996, I had a thriving business. In a review of twenty discount brokers by *Smart Money* magazine, we came in number three—not number one, true, but it gave us something to work toward. The firm earned probably $14 million before taxes; that's pretty good by most people's standards, but by the yardstick of Wall Street, it's peanuts. I felt there would be a consolidation in the industry, a bunch of mergers, and if I had a public stock, I would have the currency to get involved, to buy other firms in related or other businesses. With private stock, you don't have much to offer. I decided on a merger with a corporate "shell"—a company that no longer has an operating base (it may have been public and sold its operations out)—whose only remaining asset would be its publicly traded stock. Sometimes this is thought of as going in the back door. Although it's not a common arrangement, it is totally proper. There are always shells for sale listed in *The Wall Street Journal*. Companies may choose this option if the owners don't want to open their books or sell any of their own stock at that time, or if they don't need to raise cash, which were my reasons.

More typical is an initial public offering, which raises cash for the new company and maybe for the owners. The year before, more than five hundred companies had gone public through IPOs, raising a total of $29 billion, as opposed to only eight that went public by merging with already publicly held entities. Neither my business nor I had any immediate need for the money that would have been raised by an IPO. I could have picked up the phone and sold stock in two seconds. But I wanted to expand the business by acquisition, and I wanted the flexibility of stock to pay for those deals. I figured that sellers of rival brokerage firms or asset management companies would be more likely to accept publicly traded stock than shares in a private company.

J. Michaels Furniture was an old-line Brooklyn company with no debt, no mortgages and no lawsuits against it. But the company was going to liquidate because the pattern of furniture stores had changed. (In the past these companies had been able to make money from selling furniture; now they made money only on the high interest rates charged on installment payments.) Our mutual accountant and auditor arranged an introduction, and the owners agreed to put all their assets into a liquidating trust and buy my company. I'd end up with 97.5 percent of the new firm, which would be called Siebert Financial Corporation; the J. Michaels shareholders would get 2.5 per cent. It was a good deal—painless, efficient, an easy way to have a public float. And I was presenting the shareholders with a way to liquefy their investments; they would receive cash far in excess of the then market value, as assets including real estate were sold, and they would have a small share in my firm. Within a short time, NASDAQ passed a new set of regulations for being listed, and we did not have enough round-lot holders (with 100 shares), so we had to split the stock, which was then $10, 4 for 1, in order to retain a NASDAQ listing. The day of the split, the stock went from $10 to $16. We later offered the public shareholders the right to buy one share for each share they had at $7.50, the purpose being to see more shares publicly traded and to generate $7 million more in capital.

I was not born with a mouse in my hand. But I realized years ago that technology would be either a friend or an enemy, and in my business, I had to make it my friend. Wall Street itself had welcomed the microchip in the '60s, when computers had expedited the tedious back-office chores of recording sales, billing clients and updating portfolios. Those who wait to see which way the wind is blowing will be unfurling their sails while the competition is crossing the finish line. Embracing the brave new world of the Web, I launched SiebertNet, one of the first computerized trading venues. We do have some individuals who trade institutional-sized pieces. For that size order, which needs special handling, the broker will call the trader, who calls down to the floor and sees what's going on with the stock. If the trader noses around a little, it might get out that there are big sell orders above the market or big buy orders below the market.

Those who wait to see which way the wind is blowing will be unfurling their sails while the competition is crossing the finish line.

You're not going to get that kind of information on-line, because it's not reported on listed securities, although there is more transparency today. The way large NASDAQ orders have been handled in the last dozen years reflects Level II quotes: a compilation of the bids and offers of various market-makers at a given time within a given security. But even with Level II, buyers and sellers may not reflect the true size of orders. On listed stocks, the main market may be the NYSE, but trades can be done away from the Exchange on other markets or off the board. So order entry by computer might not be as efficient for a large working order or a thinly traded stock, but for many orders it can be done cheaper and faster because there's no live broker.

SiebertNet also made me the first self-made woman billion-aire—at least for a day, at least on paper. In February 1999 there was a lot of Internet chatter about on-line trading prospects. We had a small public float—about 10 percent of the firm's stock owned by outside investors—and there was a short squeeze because everybody was jumping on it. Shares rocketed more than 400 percent before a 4-for-1 split and the issue of new shares, designed to raise capital to improve SiebertNet. Within several weeks, shares went from $5.75 to over $70, and my 90 percent stake was worth more than a billion dollars. But the day-traders giveth and the day-traders taketh away. Fortunately, I didn't believe such a paper value. I would have gone broke when the stock started to tumble in April, had I borrowed against it. I've seen estimates of the size of losses in Internet stocks—hundreds of billions of dollars, many thousands for every man, woman and child in this country. I didn't sell any of my stock on the run-up. One day Siebert traded almost five million shares, twice the total amount of the stock in the hands of the public. I could have sold a million shares and walked away with $40 or $50 million. There's an argument to be made that I could have done good things with that much money. But would I be able to eat twice as much or wear more expensive clothes? Do I need a suite in a hotel instead of a room? I don't think those are the values that define people.

In television interviews and in my newsletter to clients, I said that the market was schizophrenic. One customer, a psychiatrist, wrote chastising me for my use of the word, saying it meant "out of reality." But the market *was* unreal. There were six times the number of companies hitting new lows as those that hit new highs on the NYSE. Yet NASDAQ companies that had little revenue and no earnings were hitting new highs every day. It didn't make sense that this was happening at the same time.

There was one story against me: The financial news Web site TheStreet.com reported that while I was telling people the Internet was a bubble and they should beware, I was selling my stock into it. *The New York Observer* reprinted the story. It was a total lie, and to prove it, I took my account statements to James Cramer (editor of the Web site) and to Arthur Carter (publisher of the paper). Cramer would not retract. The *Observer* did print a retraction—about half an inch high. I hired an attorney with the intention of suing TheStreet.com, but when I looked at the company's meager earnings (actually losses), I knew I'd never collect any money if I were to win and decided against it. As my old boss Davey Finkle used to say, "Don't get into a pissing contest with a skunk."

The technological revolution of the Internet, in my opinion, will prove to be the equivalent of the industrial revolution, and it has leveled the playing field, allowing individuals to get information at the same time as institutions. But too many new companies had a great idea with no revenues or earnings to back it up.

"Don't get into a pissing contest with a skunk."

Along with SiebertNet, I launched Mobile Broker, a high-tech interactive paging service with a keypad for investors on the go. It enables them to make stock transactions anywhere without a computer or phone.

But technology can bring dangers along with benefits. There is little accountability on the Web, and there are crooks using the Internet to pump up prices or disseminate false information. The day traders who quickly buy and sell to profit from wide daily swings in prices can be modern-day barbarians; they're influencing the market price of some companies, especially Internet stocks, along with professionals who tout stocks in Web chat rooms. It's so easy and so fascinating to trade on-line. I worry about small investors becoming addicted and obligating themselves to margin trades they might not be able to cover. If you're trading on-line, before you hit the "Send" key on an order, ask yourself if you'd write a check for that amount. There's a Wall Street cliché that should be printed on every day-trader's mouse pad: Bulls make money and bears make money, but pigs wallow.

The North American State Securities Administrators (the state regulators) estimate that Americans lose about $1 million an hour to securities fraud. When the Better Business Bureau of New York did a study on the advertising and promotional claims of discounters, it concluded that twenty-four of the twenty-nine firms had failed to state clearly how they arrived at their claims, how big a transaction was needed to receive maximum savings

---

Bulls make money and bears make money, but pigs wallow.

---

on commissions, how many clients received maximum savings or the minimum savings a customer could expect. I consider it a point of honor never to have misled a prospective client. But it's not practicable or possible to define minimum savings on a percentage basis. Our original claims were based on current full-service rates. We claimed an average of 72 percent discount, and we arrived at that figure by taking the commission charges of three leading full-service brokers, starting with 100 shares at $10 per share, all the way up to 5,000 shares at $100 per share. We made an average figure of all three firms and then compared them with our commission charges.

My momma told me: You'd better shop around. In 1994, a company called Public Sector Solutions created an advertising campaign for me, pointing to other firms that misled the public

---

My momma told me: You'd better shop around.

---

about the cost of their services. The headline of one ad read, "Honesty and integrity should never be discounted," while a TV spot urged investors to read the fine print when dealing with discount brokers that didn't charge commissions, implying that such firms made profits in other ways. Some offered deep discounts or free trades and then marked up the price of securities to make up for the loss of a full commission, or they charged excessive fees for postage or copies of statements, or they didn't sweep the cash into money market funds in a timely manner. I had a brochure printed for prospective clients on "Ten Ways to Tell if Your Discount Broker Can Be Trusted." A firm that was actually called Your Discount Broker took it personally and threatened to sue, but nothing happened. I never meant to assail that particular firm, but *The New York Times* referred to my "sledgehammer-over-the-head tactic," and I received a few irate calls from fellow brokers asking, "What the hell are you doing?" When the NASD reported complaints, I canceled the campaign. The last thing you want to do is make your regulators angry. And apparently Wall Street had something like the eleventh commandment of politics: Thou shalt not talk about thy fellow brokers. But I still feel the points I was making are valid: When I look at advertising claims, I think my ads are specific and direct, compared to the promises or implied promises of other brokers. Until it was fined, one firm ran a picture of a truck driver who

---

The last thing you want to do is make your regulators angry.

---

owned an island. How many truck drivers do you know who own islands? Some firms allow a new customer to open an account with just five hundred dollars and make twenty-five trades without paying any commission. Most customers will lose that money in their first two or three trades. Isn't that an unfair way to suck them in?

While always aware of making enemies, I didn't always know when the acrimony and ill will was gender-based. When I was still doing stock analysis, I looked into a company called Fluor Corporation that built oil refineries. It was not an industry I knew anything about, but my friend Dudley Brown at Lockheed was on the board and was impressed with the company's performance. Founder John Robert Fluor was astonished when I took notice. "Why would any institution be interested in my company?" he asked. That's a wonderful thing for a securities analyst to hear; it means bringing something new to clients. I studied the company and placed a lot of the stock with institutions. One day I got a large order and called Fluor to see if there was any stock available. He told me that he had a block of convertible preferred stock. "We bought their company," he said, "and I think the owners would like to sell some of their stock."

"Is it clean?" I asked, which means: Can it be traded?

"Absolutely," he said. Fluor's in-house lawyers said the stock was free to trade—even put the opinion in writing, and the firm's white-glove New York lawyers agreed the stock was clean. The block was converted into common shares, which I placed with a mutual fund called TV and Electronics in Chicago. I was so proud that I took out a newspaper ad to announce the trade. A few days later, I got a call from someone at the Stock Exchange, asking who had been the buyer and who the seller. That's a highly unusual kind of call, and it means trouble. Next thing I knew, I was informed that I was selling unregistered stock and was going to be censured. It wasn't until I hired a big-deal attorney who had once been the assistant to the SEC chairman that the problem disappeared. But one of Fluor's lawyers said that somebody at the Stock Exchange was out to get me. The message was clear: *Watch your step. You're playing the big boys' game now.*

Being in money management is, in a way, wonderfully empowering because statistically you can always prove what you've done. If an account starts out at $100,000 and at the end of the year that same account is worth $120,000, most clients won't care if you're male or female, black or white, Christian or Jewish or Zoroastrian. But when I entered the business, many brokerage firms were old-line WASP, and I saw quite a bit of anti-Semitism when I started to recommend my research to institutional clients. At Shields & Co., one of the partners asked me to come to his office the next day to discuss a company that I'd researched. I politely explained that I'd be taking the day off for Yom Kippur, the Jewish High Holy Day. "You can't be a member of the dill pickle and matzo ball group!" he exclaimed. When I got my seat on the Exchange, Billy Salomon, senior partner of Salomon Brothers and partner of one of the men who sponsored me, thought nothing of saying right to my face, "Too bad you don't have a little black blood in you, because you'd be quite a package." One day I happened across a greeting card that said, "Roses are reddish, Violets are bluish, In case you don't know, [open the card] I am Jewish." I bought out the entire stock. From then on, any time a client or prospective client made an anti-Semitic remark (usually after a two-martini lunch), I never said anything to embarrass him. But when I got back to the office, I'd send the card, adding, "I enjoyed lunch." I made my point and never lost a customer, or my pride.

In 1976 I bought a co-op apartment in the exclusive River House, on East Fifty-second Street. A few years later, I applied for membership in the River Club, an independent social association that had rented space in the building since 1930, with Whitneys, Roosevelts and Strawbridges as founding members. There were squash and tennis courts, a swimming pool and an elegant dining room with expansive river views. One member was known to say, "It is possible to pass through all the major cycles of life—birth, debut, marriage, anniversaries, divorce, even an affair—without once setting foot outside the River Club."

My sponsorship was impeccable, starting with Robin Chandler Duke, former president of the National Abortion and Reproductive Rights Action League and wife of Angier Biddle Duke (grandson of the founder of Duke University and ambassador to El Salvador, Spain, Denmark and Morocco). That was just the first string; my seconders were Walter Wriston (Citibank CEO) and James Robinson III (American Express CEO). I ended up on a waiting list for almost *ten* years. I thought it was distinctly curious that, out of a thousand members, only ten were Jews (one of them Henry Kissinger). There were other clubs I couldn't get into and didn't care to, but this was in the building where I live—a real convenience. The club occupied about 15 percent of the total building space but generated less than 5 percent of the revenues. I owned 320 shares of stock, or almost 1 percent of outstanding shares. I had paid $115,000 and had been offered, unsolicited but firm, close to $2.5 million; assuming my apartment was average, it meant the outstanding shares had a minimum value of around $200 million. So the value of the space occupied by the River Club could have been as high as $20 or $30 million. Tax laws permitted cooperatives to derive 20 percent of their gross income from commercial tenants who were nonstockholders. If the rent for the River Club was raised to 20 percent of the total, those of us who were tenant-owners would still be subsidizing the club, since it had not made a capital investment, and our maintenance fees would be substantially reduced. If the space was sold and the profit invested in Treasuries, which were then yielding 8 percent, our maintenance would go down 40 percent, and the value of the apartments would skyrocket. Even if three floors were sold, keeping the tennis courts, bar and restaurant for tenant-owners and investing the proceeds in Treasuries, the apartments would still jump in value because of the private amenities.

My neighbor Arthur Levitt, Jr., who went on to become SEC chairman, was on the waiting list too, although for a year or two less than I. We talked to his lawyer, who said, "You're right— you're subsidizing your neighbors." Another Jewish neighbor had been waiting about as long, and we went to see *his* lawyer, who said, "You're right, but I can't represent you because I know too many of the members." My lawyer Bill Shea and his partner, Milton Gould, eagerly agreed to take on our case pro bono. One day I saw Angie Duke in the courtyard. "Angie," I said, "I might have to sue Robin, but please don't take it personally." If I had sued and lost, I was prepared to move. I could not walk through

the door to the club, just four feet past the elevator to my apartment, and it grated. In October 1987, only two days after Black
Monday, I went to a meeting of the co-op board and explained
the inequity. I don't know whether they were all in a weakened
condition on account of seeing their investments decimated, but
the word *Jewish* was never mentioned, and everyone behaved
like ladies and gentlemen. I was elected a member of the club,
along with other residents in the building. In December the
River Club signed a new twenty-five-year lease, which would
produce more than $400,000 of increased annual income. The
announcement read: "Henceforth applications for club membership by tenant/owners will be accorded the same priority consideration as is now given near relatives of club members." Now
people of all backgrounds are admitted, even those who do not
live in the building.

Perhaps it was my own experience with prejudice and narrow-
mindedness that made me pick up the phone several years ago
when I read that the chairman of a black-owned municipal bond
firm had quit amid FBI investigations into alleged political cor-
ruption and bribes associated with a $183 million bond issue for
Dade County, Florida. He subsequently hired Johnnie Cochran
to represent him and successfully defended himself against the
charges. Nevertheless, the firm was likely to fail because no
elected official would want its municipal offerings handled by a
firm with a cloud over it.

I called the firm's other two partners, Napoleon Brandford III
and Suzanne Shank, both African-Americans, and asked them to
come in and talk with me. This wasn't a politically correct or
humanitarian gesture; the nation's urban areas were in desperate
need of repair, and somebody would have to sell bonds to
finance it. I thought that a capable firm owned by blacks and
women could have an important role. I also had a lot of respect
for their initiative with a program called COPs, or Certificates of
Participation, a form of financing widely used by municipalities.
We made a handshake deal for a limited partnership. Siebert,

Brandford, Shank & Co. celebrated its fifth anniversary in 2001 and is the paramount women- and minority-run business in the entire brokerage industry. Last year we senior-managed $2½ billion, passing several large traditional firms. But I was reminded of how little some things had changed after successfully completing our first municipal bond offering. My phone rang one night and a charming voice growled, "Mickie and her niggers," before the line went *click*.

Wall Street is the least static place in the world. You are only as good as whatever you did three minutes ago, and the world can change while you blink. But in 1999 the possibility of an initial public offering of the NYSE was earthshaking. There are broad public-policy questions raised by such a dramatic change, similar to the potential conflicts that develop when hospitals go public and have to juggle the responsibility of increasing earnings with delivering the best public health care. The capital-raising system of the United States is a national treasure. If we change it, we have to make sure it works well for the entire country. Would a public Stock Exchange start charging more for the services it provides? Would it still be able to regulate itself? Would the drive for profits affect the integrity of the system, the execution of orders? A public entity could free up more capital by selling more shares. But public companies try to increase their earnings every year; that's the name of the game. If the Stock Exchange were under that pressure, would it become a profit-making institution instead of one that serves the public and regulates its members? Could it serve two masters?

On the twenty-fifth anniversary of buying my seat, I called Bill Donaldson, the chairman of the Stock Exchange, and said that I'd like to ring the bell at the ceremonies marking the opening or closing of daily trading on the Big Board. A public relations person called me back. "Are you planning to retire?" he asked.

"Are you trying to tell me something?" I replied. But I was told that the honor of ringing the bell was reserved for people getting ready to hang up their hats. "You know what I should do instead?" I said. "I should buy a cow bell, a dinner bell and a sleigh bell, and hold a press conference."

"You wouldn't do that, would you, Mickie?" he said.

I didn't, and seven years later, the Stock Exchange made it up to me. During the last weeks of 1999, people whose influence would be felt into the next century were recognized at special bell ceremonies called "Bridging the Millennium." I was invited to ring the closing bell on December 21. I took my dog, Monster Girl, a longhaired Chihuahua, and put her on the brass platform of the balcony, but Richard Grasso, the NYSE chairman, said to me, "You'd better take her down because if she gets excited and jumps, every dog lover in America will hate us." I held her by the collar, she barked and I rang, feeling in very good company: the other ceremonial bell-ringers that week were Joe Namath, Walter Cronkite, Archbishop Desmond Tutu and Santa Claus.

10

LEAPS AND BOUNDS

*Giving back is more than an obligation,
it's a privilege.*

A few years ago, I took a long walk on a short beach and asked myself if I had the gumption and stamina to run for public office again. You've got to have fire in your belly to run and a killer instinct when tackling your opponent. The political process feels much too partisan now, but I've tried to encourage and support other female candidates whose sanguinity about making a difference remains strong. I was shocked to learn that Emily's List, a group that helps women run for office, was exclusively for pro-choice Democrats, so I became a founding member of the pro-choice Republican counterpart called WISH (Women in the Senate and House).

But however many elections are won by females, ultimately women will increase their political power only after they increase their economic power. I feel the obligation to slug it out for my gender, and I've focused on a variety of ventures where I can make a difference, never passing up the chance to speak out on issues of diversification and on the importance, the participation and the potential of women in business. In both the corporate world and as founders and owners of companies, women have been strong partners in building the American Dream. They have created nothing short of a silent revolution in our country's business life. We don't hear much about this revolution for two reasons: One is the business-as-usual focus of the financial media; the second is the almost total lack of research and analysis on the topic. Until quite recently, government data-gathering either ignored women's issues or lumped all female enterprises together as one giant monolith. Women-owned businesses today generate one out of four jobs and sell $2.3 *trillion* worth of goods annually, but this sector of the economy is virtually invisible to, and certainly unheralded by, economists and bureaucrats.

Between 1970 and 1995, the number of women aged twenty-five to fifty-four working outside the home climbed from 50 percent to 76 percent. Most of them work because they have to—many if not most families need two incomes to survive or to live well. During approximately the same time, the number of women-owned businesses increased from 5 percent to 35 percent. This explosion is dramatic across the entire nation: Even in North Dakota, the state with the slowest growth (and, frankly, not the first site we think of for feminist leaps and bounds), the number of women-owned businesses grew by nearly 40 percent from 1985 to 1996. One out of every four Americans works for a firm owned by a woman. The almost eight million women-owned companies provide more jobs in the United States than all of the Fortune 500 companies provide internationally. Every day, women start 1,600 new businesses in this country. The earnings gap in 1985—59 cents for every dollar a man made—has closed up; today it's 79 cents. I keep thinking that women are this country's secret weapon against our competitors, who do not employ women to their fullest potential.

There's an old maxim that women work harder and are superior at detail work. Female entrepreneurs are certainly working hard, but they're also exploding some myths about "traditional" women's fields: Between 1987 and 1996, the top growth industries for women-owned businesses were construction (up 171 percent), wholesale trade (up 157 percent), transportation and communications (up 140 percent), agriculture (up 130 percent) and manufacturing (up 112 percent). The highest growth rate was in larger businesses, not home-based enterprises.

The surge in women-owned businesses was an unintended consequence of the proverbial glass ceiling that corporate women discover right over their heads. But the playing field is not yet level for entrepreneurs, either. Just a few years ago, about 80 percent of the women who started businesses did it with their own personal credit cards, paying 18 or 22 percent interest—a terribly high price, unless you're making some real money. Today about half still use their credit cards for start-ups. That is twice the rate of all owners of small- and medium-sized businesses. Banks *are* starting to lend money more equitably: 46 percent of female entrepreneurs have bank credit, compared to 49 percent of their male colleagues. And their credit is good: Women-owned businesses have proved to be as financially sound and creditworthy as other U.S. firms, and they are more likely to remain in business than similar male-owned firms. When women-owned companies can get the same type of bank financing as men, I would expect to see them explode.

Mentors for women didn't exist when I started on Wall Street. Men were the hirers and firers, the promoters and demoters; a woman's presence was tolerated rather than championed. A 1972 article in *Institutional Investor* documented sporadic sightings of male sponsors but noted that women were not fooled when a man in authority lent a helping hand in building a career. "I am sure," said one securities analyst who had moved ahead with such an assist, "that men feel we do not pose as big a threat to their careers as some bright young male graduates of the Harvard Business School would." There was also a perception that the few women who made it in the rough world of finance were not concerned with sisterhood, that we preferred to preserve the exclusivity of being a woman in a man's world. The Financial Women's Association (FWA) of New York, arguably the most prestigious organization of its kind, seemed to remain silent about the Street's classic male chauvinism. "We feel that if we do a good job, it will be recognized," said its president.

In 1973 my friend Elinor Guggenheimer, then commissioner

of consumer affairs for New York City, came to me and said, "We have to start the equivalent of an old boys' network." That was the birth of the Women's Forum, now an international organization that has taken on various issues affecting working women such as elder care. Ten percent of all women who work leave their jobs at some point to take care of an elderly parent. I read one report that said if the conditions in day care centers were anything like the conditions in nursing homes, it would be a national scandal.

Another project is a task force on domestic violence. The FBI reports that two million American women are beaten each year—that's one every sixteen seconds—and the surgeon general ranked abuse by husbands and partners as the leading cause of injury to women aged fifteen to forty-four. But battered women don't always show up in emergency rooms with black eyes and broken ribs; sometimes the telltale sign is a woman who shrinks away from the innocuous human touch. Accordingly, part of the Women's Forum project is training hospital personnel to better recognize the signs of domestic violence. Abused women from the wealthiest and supposedly classiest sections of society met with us, shattering our collective conceit that wives and girl-friends who are rich enough, smart enough or successful enough are not victims of domestic violence. I heard a woman whose husband was a well-known investment banker tell how he had cut up her clothing and thrown her naked into the hallway of their apartment house. Until she finally left him, she took the freight elevator in her office building to avoid his scrutiny and punishment. My own firm had an employee who used to come to work bruised, claiming clumsiness and falls; her former husband would call the trading desk and threaten her. The first hurdle was getting her to admit the problem. The next was finding some meaningful way to intervene. We helped her change the locks on her doors and eventually move with her two children to a new apartment. But the efforts always seemed inadequate.

I've never thought money should be placed on an altar and

worshiped. What am I going to do, take it with me? I've never seen a hearse followed by a Brinks armored truck. There's much more greed permeating the financial community than in my early days, when the guys making big money gave back. Despite the cheerless welcome I received from Gus Levy when I bought my Big Board seat, he was the ultimate good citizen, turning over millions of dollars he earned as a senior partner at Goldman Sachs to Mount Sinai Hospital and raising tens of millions more. Jews call this *tzedaka*—giving back. I was taught that giving back is more than an obligation, it's a privilege. I believe in Andrew Carnegie's "gospel of wealth," which deemed surplus riches "a sacred trust to be administered for the good of the community in which it is accumulated." But I don't like handouts; I like to invest in people. When the young man who pushed the coffee cart at my office confided to me that he didn't want to remain in such a job forever, I told him, "If you'll go to computer school and send me your marks, I'll pay for it." He's a console operator now.

Margaret Thatcher once said: No one would remember the Good Samaritan if he only had good intentions. He had money as well. After the Competitive Equality Banking Act of 1987 encouraged federal institutions to direct business to women- and minority-owned firms, Siebert & Co. was invited into underwritings, and business increased by 20 percent each year. Without our status as a Women's Business Enterprise, we wouldn't have been included in most underwritings, and in 1990 I found a far-reaching way to say thank you. September 12 was my birthday. I decided to take the day off—hit some tennis balls, get a

---

No one would remember the Good Samaritan if he only had good intentions. He had money as well.

---

massage, meet a friend for lunch. But I got a call from Ruth Messinger, then the borough president of Manhattan, who was holding a press conference to launch the "Make It Shine" awards, honoring New Yorkers who were doing good things for the city. I told her I would not be going to any press conferences on my birthday, but after ten minutes of cajoling, I agreed to attend the launch.

At that ceremony, an award was given to an ex-convict who was working with children in East Harlem. The man operated out of a storefront and lived on about nine thousand dollars a year. I was sitting next to Robin Farkas, whose family had started Alexander's department stores. "If you are buying any New York City bonds in next week's offering and you give me the order," I told him, "I would like to donate my profit to this charity." That particular deal never materialized, but the idea stayed with me. I spent a quarter of a million dollars in legal fees having my attorney check the underwriting rules and tax laws on charitable gifts in all fifty states, to find out if a donation could be tied into a percentage of the commissions earned by participants in an underwriting. Corporations were permitted to donate only 5 percent of pretax income, although an entrepreneur in upstate New York later challenged the IRS on this rule and won, stating that his donations always produced business for him. I asked my lawyer and accountant to investigate, and with their approval I established the Siebert Entrepreneurial Philanthropic Plan (SEPP), which contributes to charities 50 percent of the "takedown"—the selling concession after clearing costs—that we earn from new securities. In many cases, the client chooses the charity. It's a chance to share profits from this business with organizations serving the communities from which we receive new opportunities.

No good deed goes unpunished. But there was no way I could have imagined what would happen when I tried to implement the SEPP program in New York, offering 50 percent of my gross sales commissions from the city's municipal bonds. The lead broker complained to Mayor David Dinkins that my program could prevent the city from getting the best price for the bonds.

Privately, I got a call from a senior partner of a major Wall Street firm who said accusingly, "You're just doing this to embarrass us." I had picked seven charities that would be the beneficiaries of the bond sales. The mayor said my orders would be honored, but there would be no conference at City Hall to announce the program.

I waited six months before calling the highest-ranking woman in munies at First Boston, which had underwritten the bonds, and asked to meet with the senior partners. "I could take all the energy in my life and all the money I've made," I said, "and I couldn't change the course of a $1.3 billion underwriting. I was hoping I could make you guys understand why I'm doing this." She invited me to come speak to her colleagues. I talked about being given an opportunity as a woman and wanting to give something back. I thought I did a pretty good job. Then the First Boston woman gave me a report: "You should have heard them when you left," she said. "They were furious."

SEPP was later expanded to include the underwriting of all municipal, government and corporate new-issue securities. In 1991, the program's first full year, donations totaled more than $300,000. During the first two years, more than fifty charities across the country benefited: the Boys and Girls Clubs of Boston, which run youth guidance programs at three club-houses; the National Alliance to End Homelessness, headquartered in Washington, D.C., which coordinates support for the homeless nationwide; God's Love We Deliver, an organization that distributes free meals to homebound AIDS patients in the New York City area; the Hearing Dog Program of Minnesota, which trains dogs to assist the hearing-impaired; and the Austin, Texas, affiliate of Habitat for Humanity, which arranges no-interest mortgages for volunteer-built homes that go to needy families.

It was gratifying to get thank-you notes that told about the real results of these donations. A $25,000 check to City Harvest in New York purchased a vehicle that would deliver more than

150,000 pounds of food to the needy for six months; $5,567 to the Senior Resources Division of Volunteers of America in Minneapolis helped preserve the independence of elderly citizens; $12,473 to the German School of New York, in White Plains, meant a sports facility for 340 students; $2,500 to Boston's Orchard Park Neighborhood House financed a summer program for inner-city youths; $2,923 to WEAVE (Women Escaping a Violent Environment) provided shelter for 779 victims of family violence in Sacramento, California, including 450 children.

In 1992 I was driving a rental car through the riot-damaged sections of South-Central Los Angeles, and I was shocked by what I saw: buildings burned down, the rubble not even cleared yet. It had been the destruction of an inner city at the hands of the very people who lived there. Small, struggling businesses had been decimated by the upheaval. I had SEPP money and proposed to some institutions that if they designated Siebert & Co. for new issues, we would use 50 percent of the gross sales commission to start the L.A. Women's Entrepreneurial Fund. Our aim was to provide a fresh source of money for female business owners who couldn't get loans from traditional sources to rebuild and reopen their businesses because they didn't have credit histories. More than fifty candidates were submitted for the initial loans of between $1,000 and $15,000. On Wall Street, we see money being made outside any sense of reality, money that I never knew existed. It's easy to forget that sometimes a few thousand dollars can spell the difference between a person's being self-sufficient and being on welfare.

Young Sook Park ran a swap meet that was looted and destroyed five days after she'd opened; Rina Men's beauty salon had its equipment either stolen or destroyed; Lillian Mobley's mailbox rental and copier service was shut down because adjacent stores were burning; a Hmong needlework artist named See Lee lost all of her materials. When Mayor Tom Bradley came to the press conference announcing the loan, he reminisced about his days as a police officer at the nearby Newton Street station—

how he would sneak away for homemade sweet potato pies at the bakery that had been in Alberta Craven's family for fifty years. Now her husband drove the delivery van, and her daughter, an Olympic gold medalist in track, handled collections because, she said, the debtors couldn't outrun her. But their operation too had been destroyed in the rioting.

The Entrepreneurial Fund, administered without charge by the California Community Foundation, set up a flexible repayment schedule for the women and promised a 2 percent discount at the end of the loan term as reward for prompt payment. (The needlework artist paid us back in one- and five-dollar bills.) An organization called Rebuild L.A. did follow up with the women to find other sources of help for business development and expansion. Mine was the only woman-owned firm in the sale of General Motors stock to the public at the time, and I promised Mayor Bradley that if any clients participating in the SEPP program selected Rebuild L.A. as their charity of choice, I would contribute 100 percent of our commissions on those transactions. I donated $150,000 from the GM revenues and did the same thing with Chrysler. Having seen the riot damage, I knew I didn't want to make a damn cent from it.

In February 1993, the terrorist bombing of the World Trade Center damaged hundreds of businesses, large and small. Many of them were in desperate need of basic services—telecommunications, relocation and access to information. That August, I donated $100,000 to launch the Business Emergency Fund in New York, a program that awarded grants of up to $1,000 to small businesses to help offset the costs associated with restoration or relocation caused by fire, flood, riot, blackout or civil disturbance. The funds would be available within twenty-four hours.

We still tell clients about SEPP, but the program never took off the way it should have—a big disappointment when I thought we'd be donating $5 million to $10 million a year. The economic well-being of New York is dependent in part on the city's ability to respond to the needs of business, particularly in difficult times. So the real question that should be asked is not why I did this, but why didn't anybody else? Take stands, take risks, take responsibility.

When I was growing up, children were taught how to save. We got savings stamps from a vending machine, put them in a pass-book and took them to a bank. That kind of discipline doesn't exist today, at home or in schools. As superintendent of banking, I reconfirmed what I had learned during my first year in business, when I found that people—especially women people—didn't have basic financial information. I became sensitive to the

Take stands, take risks, take responsibility.

little guys, as well as the people with more assets, who just didn't know about things like IRAs or Keoghs, or adjustable- or fixed-rate mortgages, let alone the more complicated financial products and services available to them. Everyone should have general economic knowledge: If you don't know what the Federal Reserve does, then you can't understand how an increase in interest rates affects the economy, the nation's business, your investments and maybe your mortgage. In the last century, immigrants entering the workforce could function financially with just a bank account. Today, personal finance is much more complicated.

In 1998 I won the Sara Lee Frontrunners Award, honoring the service, accomplishments and abilities of women. I've received a lot of awards, and they boost my ego, but I think they serve the larger social purpose of making the world aware that women are achievers in every field of endeavor. (The other Frontrunners were the novelist Isabel Allende, Secretary of Health and Human Services Donna Shalala and Elaine Jones, the first African-American woman elected to the American Bar Association Board of Governors.) The following spring, I arranged to have the $50,000 prize money go to the youth organization Girls Incorporated, which helped to underwrite a curriculum about financial literacy. When I was superintendent of banking, among the industries I regulated were the check cashers and licensed lenders. I saw firsthand that those who could least afford these services paid more.

When I became president of the New York Women's Agenda, I told the board at the first meeting that my project would be developing a program to teach high school students the fundamentals of personal finance. Jo LoCicero, a board member, raised her hand and said, "I can help you. I taught in the school system for thirty years." She set up a meeting with the chancellor, Rudy Crew, and within eight weeks we had an outline of the program. It was tested in two large public high schools in each of the five boroughs of New York City, as well as selected Virtual Enterprise Schools (those high schools that have as part of their curriculum the running of a simulated business by students). The course covered basic financial information—how to manage checking accounts, the uses and abuses of credit cards. I was astonished to hear from one teacher about a young student with a part-time job who had brought her his paycheck, complaining that some of his money had been "stolen." No one had taught him about taxes. These kids didn't understand that by charging last night's dinner on a credit card and paying the minimum balance, they would be paying for that meal for the next fifteen years. We are currently expanding the program and hope that it will soon be in every New York city high school. My goal is that every student graduating from high school will be required to take one basic course in finance that would include credit cards, bank accounts, different types of mortgages, retirement accounts and the advantages and disadvantages of buying or leasing a car. These are tools that real people need to get the most out of their money.

• • •

For almost fifty years, I've been fighting, dodging and trying to derail the deeply ingrained misogyny of the financial community. Harvard Business School graduated its first woman in the 1940s, but progress since then has been glacial. And it isn't all about money. Women on Wall Street earn far more than those in other industries, and this "golden muzzle" of high compensation makes being even a token woman on Wall Street attractive. The real issue is about being able to have meaningful, decision-making roles.

In 1985 a letter was sent to the deans of the nation's leading business schools by a group at Goldman Sachs known as the Antidiscriminatory Underground. These women were all well paid, earning annual salaries between $50,000 and $250,000, but their letter alleged that women were not allowed into the inner sanctum of Goldman Sachs. Compensation of the top women was a fraction of that of the top men; there were no women partners; and there was a pervasive discriminatory attitude. One Goldman Sachs associate on a recruiting foray at Stanford University actually asked female candidates, "Would you have an abortion rather than jeopardize your career?" When this incident was made public in *The Wall Street Journal,* the banker was reprimanded but not fired. One year after the Underground's letter-writing campaign, in October 1986, Jeanette Loeb became the first female partner of Goldman Sachs; Morgan Stanley named three women managing directors (equal to partner); and Salomon promoted a woman to managing director.

When *BusinessWeek* ran an article about the Underground's letter, I was called for a comment. "If men are made partners in ten years," I asked, "why isn't the same standard used for women?" One of the partners at Goldman Sachs later told me that I had forced him to think about the process of interviewing women in business school. He said that two or three partners, when they questioned themselves, believed that they tended to look for the qualities they admired in their mothers, sisters or wives—totally different qualities from those they sought in men.

Today things have changed somewhat at Goldman Sachs, and women become partners regularly.

Just like the Supreme Court justice who couldn't define pornography but knew it when he saw it, I know what does *not* constitute progress. In August 1989 *Playboy* magazine published an article by Louis Rukeyser on the women of Wall Street. It began with the story of me buying the NYSE seat despite Gus Levy's saying "We don't want her" and "We have no ladies' room on the floor." The following half-dozen pages were devoted to photos of women who worked in finance, bare-breasted and open-crotched (one was lying on sheets printed with stock market stats). All but one had left their companies, voluntarily or laid off, by the time the pictorial was published.

When *Life* magazine was doing a special issue on the Stock Exchange, I wrote to the managing editor asking him not to use a photograph of me standing in front of a male urinal. I had done it as a joke for a book on the two hundredth anniversary of the Big Board. The photographer was quite persuasive, saying, "This will be funny because of all that talk about your bathroom habits when you bought the seat." But when that was the *only* picture used, I was hugely embarrassed. The idea of not having a place to pee diminished the importance of my efforts to achieve equality for women in the financial community, and I regretted posing for it. The picture kept coming back to haunt me; of course *Life* used it.

A new generation of women has been able to do well in money management. During the 1990s, Abby Joseph Cohen, the chief market strategist for Goldman Sachs, was called "the Prophet of Wall Street," owing her success to examination of quarterly earnings reports by every company in the Standard & Poor's 500. The financial community reacted as a monolith to her view that traditional benchmarks of stock market valuation—price-earnings ratios, dividend rates and margin debt balances—are of little use today. This was heady influence, indeed, for someone who commuted to work from her home in Queens on a city bus and did her own laundry. Mary Meeker, the Internet analyst at Morgan Stanley, was called "The Oracle of the Net." Her predictions about stocks based on their first-in-line advantage in an explosive new medium (rather than traditional stock valuations based on earnings) helped pull the tech-heavy NASDAQ into record territory in the '90s. Recommendations—even raised eyebrows—from these two women could send stocks soaring or sliding. If power, as Hewlett-Packard CEO Carly Fiorina said, is the ability to change things, these women had power, at least until the free fall of tech stocks. As one of the chief cheerleaders for these now-deflated stocks, Meeker was blamed for misleading the public and has lost her stature; Cohen came under attack for wrong calls, but she has predicted major market moves and occupies a unique position on Wall Street.

A recent article in *Institutional Investor* said that true equality will arrive the day a woman with mediocre abilities heads an investment bank. But I think equality will come only when women who gain power on the Street begin to use it on behalf of other women. Lawsuits won't do it. It will take the decided

---

You either take the challenges that present themselves or not, and none of us has any guarantees.

---

effort of major firms to make sure that women are advanced according to their abilities, and it will be up to the women who rise to the top to see that they make that effort. That's a bit of a catch-22, not unlike what occurred more than thirty years ago when the NYSE insisted that a bank agree to lend me $300,000 for my seat, and the bank said no unless the Exchange made me a commitment.

I don't know if I've ever broken into the old boys' network, but I've survived without it, and a lot of people who didn't accept me at first learned to respect me. Because I was a woman, I probably had to work harder, but because I was the first, it became a challenge. You go one of two ways in this world: You either take the challenges that present themselves or not, and none of us has any guarantees. I remember one time when I was running like mad for a taxi in the rain. When I got into the backseat, I said, "Thank God you're here—it's such a lousy morning." The cabbie turned to me with a look of exasperation. "Lady!" he practically yelled. "There is *no such thing* as a lousy morning. You are not *owed* today." I've kept that thought with me, and if I ever see that cabbie again, I will take out all the money in my wallet and give it to him.

Perhaps it's progress that some women are developing reputations as bulldogs: In a *New York Times Magazine* article, a finance executive at E. F. Hutton attributed her success to her ability to "slug down stingers till dawn" with clients. The day of the boozy business lunch is past, but when I was coming up, part of the job involved matching a client scotch for scotch. The only time my family drank liquor was at funerals (when someone would take a straight shot and then grimace) or as an antidote to a cold (schnapps). But on the Street, I developed something of a reputation for being a two-fisted drinker. (I also ate meat three times a day. Times change.) But I never drank alone at home. I'd

---

> "There is *no such thing* as a lousy morning.
> You are not *owed* today."

---

go to a neighborhood restaurant for a drink before dinner. In my generation, there was a scarcity of men secure enough to handle a woman hitting the headlines, and when you're coming up fast, you find that you outgrow people along the way. And I wanted to have fun, not talk business, at night. (I used to take vacations with a girlfriend who was the first woman officer of a prominent investment company; we had a deal that the first one who talked stocks, bonds or business had to fork over a dollar, to be used toward our predinner drinks.)

Some people I met socially would trawl for "inside informa-

tion," so I'd play the dumb blonde at parties. I started on Wall
Street giving investment advice to clients, but I wouldn't give my
best friend a tip. Unrealistic expectations could destroy a friend-
ship. There are smart men who are tickled to death with an
annual 20 percent return on their business but expect stocks to
double in a month. It makes more sense to think of the money
you put in the stock market entrepreneurially: If you owned a
business that showed a 20 percent profit on invested capital in a
year, you'd be pleased. If it broke even some months, or even
showed a loss, you'd just work harder. So it is with common
stocks: You can't expect to double your money in a year any
more than you can expect to lose twenty pounds by the end of
the week—not unless you have a reliable crystal ball. Brokers
don't know everything. If we did, we'd all be sitting at home
clipping coupons rather than coming to work. And there are
valid differing opinions: Whenever I crossed a block of stock, by
definition it meant that somebody thought the price was too
high and somebody else thought it was too cheap. There can be
many reasons for a transaction.

Alan Greenspan may be akin to a rock star, but people don't
like to hear the hard, unsexy truth about the market. Successful
investing in the stock market is like a marriage, not an affair.
Many investors are like couples who began with little else other
than good prospects but applied principles of constancy, sharing
the times of stress and tribulation. When they were courting,

---

**Brokers don't know everything. If we did, we'd
all be sitting at home clipping coupons
rather than coming to work.**

---

they looked for qualities in each other that would stand up well
and enhance in value over the years—not just an appealing phys-
iognomy but a sound mind, a sense of purpose, a potential for
growth.

You can fall in love with a company but not with the stock.

The Enron scandal notwithstanding, big companies are usually safer than small companies, but they may or may not be better investments. In the 1970s, Wall Street pros believed in the "Nifty Fifty": blue-chip companies such as IBM, Xerox, Polaroid, Avon and Disney that were thought to be security blankets. Even if you bought at a high, went the reasoning, sooner or later the price would be justified by these premier growth stocks. But inevitably, as *Forbes* magazine columnist Martin Sosnoff put it, they were taken out and shot one by one. Disney had trouble

You can fall in love with a company but not with the stock.

obtaining gas during an oil embargo. Polaroid's new cameras had production problems. Avon reeled after a critical cover story in *Forbes*. The late 1990s created a lot of overpriced stocks—the same problem we saw accelerating in early 2001. Certain stocks were selling based not on predictable growth but on unrealistic dreams.

You can hardly go wrong if you invest in sound, well-financed companies that are leaders in industries growing faster than the economy as a whole, but they must continue to grow. Investors refer to it as GARP: growth at a reasonable price. You should probably start to invest through mutual funds if you don't have the stomach to pick up the paper or turn on CNBC-TV and find out you've lost that day. If you don't invest, your money is not

You can hardly go wrong if you invest in sound, well-financed companies that are leaders in industries growing faster than the economy as a whole, but they must continue to grow.

working aggressively for you. Money in the bank works to one degree, but money in stocks is capable of working to another degree. Bonds and munies work in yet another way, as do con-

vertibles. Most stocks are too big to be manipulated. A brokerage's recommendation might influence the price, but stocks are
self-leveling. You can't keep a good stock down or a bad one up.
Successful investors need money, patience and logic, in that
order. Luck influences everything you do, but you can reduce the
role of luck with good fundamental research.

Trading off the tape is like betting on horses, and listening to
a "tip" is not investing, it's speculating, which involves taking a
much larger risk. Taking the advice of friends, whether conservative or speculative, is worse than doctoring yourself—it's letting another rank amateur doctor you. If you want to take a

---

You can't keep a good stock down or a bad one up.

---

chance on some wild things, do it with no more than 10 percent
of your cash. Then you'll be gambling at "sleeping level," rather
than pacing the floor at 3:00 A.M. with hot milk and Zantac. But
the quality of research that's available to individuals today is ter-
rific. For ten dollars you can get almost everything on a company. The Thompson Corporation's First Call global research
network is a great compilation of analysts' earnings estimates. It
was originally designed for institutions, and they pay dearly for
it, but now individual investors can get a bargain, paying a few

---

**Trading off the tape is like betting on horses,
and listening to a "tip" is not investing,
it's speculating.**

---

dollars for numbers from an independent research source. What
I'd call "maintenance" on an investment might involve reading
earnings reports for the company three or four times a year. If
you are computer-literate, the Internet has leveled the playing
field. Solid information on companies is available to anyone. But
if you put your money in stocks that are just today's game, if
you've bought stock on a "story" or on its momentum, you have

to watch it closely. If a stock doubles, for instance, and you find that the reasons you liked the stock are still there, you can be conservative and sell half, to get your cost out. If you expect a slowdown in earnings, sell more. Some stocks can't afford even small earnings disappointments. If the disappointment is because the company had a delay and is going to ship a product in July instead of May, it could be a buying opportunity if you know the product is good. But sometimes you have to respond. The company might make more money than people thought, but the stock still doesn't do anything because the market can react to a disappointment.

In 1998 I got a call from the police asking if I knew anybody named Sante or Kenneth Kimes. The mother-and-son grifters who would later be convicted of the murder of a wealthy elderly New Yorker named Irene Silverman apparently had made a list of potential victims—and my name was on it—compiled from an inventory of people who owned condominiums at the Palm Beach Polo and Country Club in Wellington, Florida. (I'd sold it because the location was so remote.) It wasn't the first time that having a public profile made me a target of criminals. When Ed Koch was mayor, I'd asked for police protection because a crazy man was sending me his semen wrapped in a napkin. (My request was refused.) And Assistant District Attorney Linda Fairstein, head of the Manhattan Sex Crimes Unit, called me when the same man was arrested for raping a woman in the Helmsley Palace Hotel. He was muttering that his problems would be over if he married a rich Jewish woman. This man had my name and phone number in his wallet and used to call me, saying that he was waiting for me to come downstairs.

I've sacrificed privacy, but I've enjoyed the public acclamation. Money is better than poverty, if only for financial reasons (can't take credit for that line—it was Woody Allen's). But more important is personal freedom. I don't have to go to a boss or senior

> ## Money is better than poverty, if only
> ## for financial reasons.

partner and ask, "May I?" That means a lot to me. There are people who will run screaming from the room at the mention of my name, but I sleep well at night, knowing that I've been competitive but honest, tenacious but scrupulous, tough but fair. And I guess I've enjoyed my toughness.

A few years ago, my five-pound Chihuahua tore away from her leash and tried to tackle my neighbor Henry Kissinger's 100-pound Labrador in the lobby of the apartment building where

> ## I sleep well at night, knowing that I've been
> ## competitive but honest, tenacious but
> ## scrupulous, tough but fair.

we both live. As I tried to pull her away, I slipped on wet marble and fell, tearing ligaments in my thumb. I was telling that story to Mario Cuomo, gesticulating with my hand, which was still in a cast from the surgery.

"Governor," I said, "the dog doesn't know her own size."

"Mickie," he replied, "that dog belongs to you."

AFTERWORD:
MUST GREED BE THE CREED?

In recent years, the financial markets have been as dramatic as the wider world they reflect. During the 1990s, as millions of new jobs were created, Wall Street responded; the stock market increased by more than double digits year after year. Techies were the glamour kids of the new economy, and the lure of getting in on the ground floor of a new company in a dynamic new industry was exciting, promising big and fast wealth. For the first time, leading investment banks financed dot-com start-ups, a role traditionally reserved for well-established companies. And as the tech companies went public, some of them tripling in value on their first day of trading, instant millionaires were created. But many of the NASDAQ stocks that reached daily new highs had little revenue and no profits. (Alan Greenspan of the Federal Reserve Bank called this speculative bubble "irrational exuberance.") On the Big Board, for each stock that hit a new high, there were five that sank to new lows. When it was realized that there were almost no revenues or earnings for many dot-coms, and the companies were failing, the founders of some companies sold stock worth hundreds of millions of dollars, leaving stockholders with worthless securities.

In August 1998 a powerful hedge fund called Long-Term Capital Management (whose illustrious rostrum of partners included two Nobel Prize winners) had to be rescued from bankruptcy by the Fed, which used its power to coerce Wall Street firms and banks to take over this failing institution. Using derivatives and buying on margin played a major part in this near disaster. Two months later, I testified before the Committee on Banking and Financial Services of the House of Representatives, proposing two courses of action. It was essential that disclosure of derivative positions be increased and that the United States take a leadership role in establishing global margin and reporting regulations for derivatives and margins. Had these ideas been implemented, the recent debacle at Enron might have been averted, and innocent investors and employees might have avoided significant financial losses.

It was only weeks after the national tragedy of September 11, 2001, when the World Trade Center crumbled into oblivion, that Enron became front-page news. The company, which had started out operating a natural gas pipeline, had been regarded as the tenth largest in the country, with an enviable record. It had reported $101 billion in revenues in the year 2000, with a market capitalization of $63 billion and a stock price as high as $90 per share. But in October 2001, Enron announced that it would take a $35 million charge-off to earnings to reflect losses in partnerships that were off the balance sheet, the details of which had never been revealed to either individuals or institutional holders. More than $1 billion in shareholder equity would be wiped out. The following week, the SEC started investigating Enron's accounting practices, and from then on, the downturn was quick. The stock plunged 60 percent, and the company exhausted its line of credit. (With the exception of $1 billion from Citibank and JP Morgan Chase, Enron was turned down by every other source of capital.) Previously reported net income dating back to 1997 was reduced by $586 million, or 20 percent, and Enron's credit rating was lowered to a "B" by Standard & Poor's. The knockout punch came when the new junk rating forced the company to immediately repay almost $4 billion in debts owned by its "Special Purpose Entities"—those partnerships with a tiny percentage not owned by

Enron and therefore not legally required to be consolidated on the company's financials.

In late November 2001, Enron filed for bankruptcy—the largest in U.S. history. Investors learned for the first time about "debt triggers," written into the terms of a bond issue but not usually disclosed to the public. Employees were not permitted to sell the stock that they had been encouraged to buy for their retirement plans and had to watch as it plummeted in value. Many of these people are now jobless and broke, while Enron's top officers realized hundreds of millions of dollars of profit selling their shares. Certainly the employees, not to mention the public, would not have invested in the company had they known that Enron was operating by legal loopholes and financial engineering. An article in *The New York Times* revealed that if Enron had used the accounting standards employed by most companies, it would not have been ranked the tenth largest in the country; it would have been number 287.

As Enron imploded, the shocking decay of business ethics emerged. Enron represents a total moral bankruptcy. How did so many highly respected professionals—the accountants, the lawyers, the commercial bankers and Wall Street firms—abuse the trust that had been placed with them and create this historic mess? How did so many people ignore basic values? What happened to their integrity? And why didn't the normal checks and balances work? Was the money just so big and the culture so twisted?

When I was superintendent of banking, I realized that regulations could not keep up with fast-moving technological advances. It is my hope that there will be a new set of regulations and laws created by the SEC and Congress to eliminate the loopholes and set the pattern for fairness for the investing public. The new laws should cover:

• Transparency: easy-to-understand financial statements, clearly disclosing off-balance-sheet items

- Timely reporting of important corporate events
- Disclosure by directors and officers, within two or three business days, of any personal transactions in the stock or securities of the company—including derivatives
- Disclosure of any trigger in the corporate debt or the company's financial position that could have a significant effect on the stock
- Disclosure of recommendations, positions, personal holdings and income based on investment banking relationships of analysts
- Disclosure of derivative positions—reporting requirements needed on a global basis
- Meaningful penalties for violations
- New rules for 401(k) retirement accounts

In connection with 401(k) retirement accounts, many Americans have seen their nest eggs devastated since March 2000, and most notoriously by the scandals affecting some of our largest corporations. On August 6, 2002, I urged in a *New York Times* op-ed piece that the government make a commitment to double—for three to five years—the amount that investors can put into their 401(k) plans and individual retirement accounts (IRAs). It seemed to me so urgent that we change the rules, that I was grateful to be able to discuss this issue directly with top government leaders in Washington, and, on August 13, 2002, to speak at President Bush's Economic Forum in Waco, Texas, to present this recommendation personally.

I have great faith in the technological creativity of this country. Our capital-raising system became too enthusiastic and needs fine-tuning now, but it is unique and is the envy of the world. If the changes we need are implemented, we'll be able to look back ten years from now and view today's financial events merely as an unfortunate episode of history. And I will be able to say to both investors and young people coming to Wall Street: Welcome.

ACKNOWLEDGMENTS

I could not express a proper thank-you without mentioning my parents, Dr. Irwin J. and Margaret Roseman Siebert. Many times when I have done something out of the ordinary, my thoughts have turned to them, and I'm sorry that they were not here to share it with me.

Bache & Co.'s Monte Gordon and Steve Joseph gave me my first job. Ed Merkle, president of the Madison Fund, gave me my first order, and I learned how to handle large orders from Davie Finkle. I am profoundly grateful to former New York governor Hugh Carey, who appointed me superintendent of banking, which gave me the chance to see financial markets from a different perspective.

One night at a dinner given at Manhattan's Museum of Television and Radio, I sat next to Lou Weiss, chairman of the board, emeritus, of the William Morris Agency. "I've followed your career," he said. "You should have a book in you." When I said yes, he had the agent Mel Berger call. Mel, in turn, introduced me to Aimee Lee Ball, who was of enormous help in putting my thoughts on paper. Fred Hills of The Free Press is a great taskmaster.

June Jaffee, my dearest friend, is helping with my financial literacy school program. If I am successful and this program becomes national, it will probably be the most important thing I've ever done.

INDEX

Printed in the United States
By Bookmasters